STRENGTH

Published by SuccessBooks®, Lake Mary, FL.

SuccessBooks® is a registered trademark.

ISBN: 979-8-9892734-9-2
LCCN: 2024920805

This publication is designed to provide accurate and authoritative information with regard to the subject matter covered. It is sold with the understanding that the publisher is not engaged in rendering legal, accounting, or other professional advice. If legal advice or other expert assistance is required, the services of a competent professional should be sought. The opinions expressed by the authors in this book are not endorsed by SuccessBooks® and are the sole responsibility of the author rendering the opinion.

Scripture quotations marked ESV are from The ESV® Bible (The Holy Bible, English Standard Version®), copyright © 2001 by Crossway, a publishing ministry of Good News Publishers. Used by permission. All rights reserved.

Scripture quotations marked KJV are from the King James Version of the Bible.

Scripture quotations marked NIV are taken from the Holy Bible, New International Version®, NIV®. Copyright © 1973, 1978, 1984, 2011 by Biblica, Inc.® Used by permission of Zondervan. All rights reserved worldwide. www.zondervan.com. The "NIV" and "New International Version" are trademarks registered in the United States Patent and Trademark Office by Biblica, Inc.®

Scripture quotations marked NKJV are taken from the New King James Version®. Copyright © 1982 by Thomas Nelson. Used by permission. All rights reserved.

Most SuccessBooks® titles are available at special quantity discounts for bulk purchases for sales promotions, premiums, fundraising, and educational use. Special versions or book excerpts can also be created to fit specific needs.

For more information, please write:

SuccessBooks®
3415 W. Lake Mary Blvd. #950370
Lake Mary, FL 32795
or call 1.877.261.4930

Visit us online at: www.CelebrityPressPublishing.com.

STRENGTH

CRUSH FEAR,
EMBRACE CHANGE,
ACHIEVE SUCCESS

SUCCESS
BOOKS®
Lake Mary, FL

CONTENTS

CHAPTER 16

From Impossible to Inevitable

Listening to Silent Stakeholders

CHAPTER 1

KEEPING THE FAITH

Anchors of Strength to Carry You Through Life

By Kathy Ireland

I didn't see it coming.

That's the nature of life's curveballs.

There had been rumors, of course, but I was still shocked to hear that the debris from the bankruptcy of a forty-billion-dollar retail giant could directly fall onto my family.

While many know me as a model, I've always been an entrepreneur! I started selling painted rocks at just four years old and became one of our town's very first paper girls when I was 11 1/2. The world of business excited me, and modeling was never the plan. When the opportunity to model was presented, I saw it as a vehicle to pay for school and to fund the many business ideas I had mulling around in my mind.

When the modeling career began to simmer, I took the money I'd saved and started kathy ireland Worldwide from my kitchen table. Soon, I was approached by a company that wanted me to promote its socks. I knew intuitively that a better plan was to go into business with this sock maker and start our brand. We sold more than one hundred million pairs! We entered an exclusive contract with Kmart, and our brand became a household name. When I first started the company, we slept in airports instead of hotel rooms to save money, but soon we had the freedom to loosen the purse strings a bit! I believed we were in a contract that guaranteed security, so my team and I were enjoying our success.

That's when the sucker punch landed!

I was called to a meeting, and with a chilling smile, the banker told me that the retailer we were totally dependent on was in major financial trouble. If they filed for bankruptcy, the entire liability would fall on me. "We can take your house," he said with zero compassion, "and the houses of all your business partners."

At that time, we had thirty-seven people with families on our team who were dependent on us for their paychecks. I found the strength to persevere. I wasn't about to abandon our partners at Kmart during their worst time, so we supported them while they navigated what became the largest retail bankruptcy of all time.

Not only did our brand survive, but we went on to become a *multibillion*-dollar company that *Women's Wear Daily* called the highest-ranking woman-owned licensing business in American history!

I worked hard to get here yet didn't do it alone. Yes, I have an amazing team of brilliant people; however, my strongest business partner, the one I turn to when I need an infusion of strength and wisdom, is Jesus.

Philippians 4:13 says, "I can do all things through Christ who strengthens me" (NKJV).

It's true! I don't know how I would have navigated that terrible period were it not for my relationship with Jesus. However, I didn't find Him in a church.

I had found Him years earlier in a Paris apartment.

STRENGTH IN FAITH

At eighteen years old I went to Paris to begin a modeling career. I stayed at the bright, beautifully ornate Parisian apartment of my agent. In contrast, my room was at the end of a long, dark, narrow hallway. I would later understand why other girls referred to that room as the dungeon. It was shocking when my agent's husband tried to kiss me in the elevator. I escaped from him and spent as little time as possible in that apartment, always going right to the "dungeon" and locking the door.

One night I noticed a Bible tucked into my suitcase.

Mom.

I believed in God, yet didn't have a relationship with Him, and Mom's faith was relatively new. She was a nurse, and while she was in school, she befriended a woman who, like her, had three daughters but always seemed to be grounded in grace and peace.

One day Mom said to her, "I don't get it. You have three young daughters, and I have three young daughters, yet you seem totally at peace! How?"

The woman replied, "Jesus."

From that day on, Mom became a devoted follower of Jesus. I noticed she was stronger and more confident. Still as a self-absorbed teenager, I didn't pay much attention to the root of that change.

That night in the "dungeon," however, I opened to the Gospel of Matthew and started reading. Suddenly, I knew what I was reading was the truth, and from that day on, Jesus was my Lord and Savior.

That relationship gave me strength to walk away from jobs that felt at variance to what I knew of Scripture. Yet, my rebellion caused me to cherry-pick the Bible. I would cling to certain verses and dismiss others as irrelevant to me. In pride and ignorance, I avoided the vast majority of God's Word for decades to come. That arrogance led to me making many, many mistakes. Scripture tells us the one who is forgiven much, loves much. I love a whole bunch!

It's never too late or too early to give God His rightful position of first place in our lives. Surrendering to Him is the epitome of strength.

No matter your past, no matter your circumstances, please know you are valuable, you are loved, and you matter. God made you and He doesn't make mistakes.

Matthew 19:26 says, "Jesus looked at them and said, 'With man this is impossible, but with God all things are possible'" (NIV).

I would need to call on that faith many times in life when I felt lost, when I was overwhelmed, and years later, when I came face-to-face with a deadly predator.

STRENGTH IN CONFRONTING THE ENEMY

In the early '90s my husband and I visited a friend in Fiji. We called him Captain Adrian, and he took us scuba diving off the coasts of beautiful remote islands. He warned us that the only sharks we needed to worry about were the bronze whalers, but we didn't expect to see any.

When scuba diving, you pair up with a buddy, someone you can signal to if you're in trouble. My buddy was Captain Adrian. We were about one hundred feet deep, and just as he turned his back to me, I saw a bronze whaler shark coming my way. He swayed back and forth, taunting me, but I remembered my training. Never turn your back on a predator! When he swayed, I swayed. I did everything I could to make myself appear bigger and more threatening, and as he moved closer, I stood my ground. I turned my head for one second to try to alert Captain Adrian to my predicament. In that instant I heard the boom of the spear gun. He had shot the shark. I didn't want the shark to be killed, but I was told that the second I took my eyes off him, he lunged toward me.

It wouldn't be the last time I was hunted by a predator!

In business the sharks are always circling. The bigger your goals and visibility, the more sharks you'll encounter and the more diligent you have to be about staring them down.

I was once asked to host the red carpet at the Oscars right after returning from a mission trip to Haiti. I'd just seen so much devastation and was then thrust into the contrasting glitz and glam of the awards show. I did my best, but it was out of my comfort zone. During the broadcast, someone tweeted that I looked like I was on drugs and that whoever hired me should be killed. I did the research and found out that the man who wrote the tweet was CMO of one of the largest marketing firms in the world. I tweeted back, reminding him that I was a human being and condemning his incendiary comment. He apologized, removed the tweet, and when I called him later, he picked up.

He was mortified and sheepishly admitted that from behind the computer, he felt anonymous enough to say whatever he wanted. We had a good conversation, and I even asked him how I might improve.

When someone attacks, resist the urge to run, resist the urge to counterattack, and instead, stand strong. Confront the critics and the bullies in such a way that they lose their power over you.

In Romans 8:31 it says, "If God be for us, who can be against us?" (KJV).

When the shark comes at you, find the thread of humanity between you, ask questions, learn from them, and don't let who *they* are change who *you* are. Stand tall; hold them accountable. Your character might teach *them* a lesson or two.

STRENGTH IN HUMILITY

As the business grew, the media came calling.

The problem was I had a very squeaky, childlike voice. I couldn't even order a pizza. The pizza shop would ask to speak to my parents! That didn't matter when I was modeling and the job was to "shut up and pose," but now that I had a chance to speak publicly, I felt exposed. One critic said my voice could kill small animals.

It was hurtful to read, but I pressed on. I was asked to do a speaking engagement with Ernst and Young. Still very introverted, I peeked out of the curtain from backstage and saw the people filing in. I wanted to run, but one of my business partners set me straight!

He said to me, "You're uncomfortable. But these people paid money for this; they organized childcare to be here; they paid for transportation. Your discomfort is irrelevant. You have information to share that will help them, and that's what you're going to do!"

It was a reminder to take my eyes off myself.

Philippians 2:3 says, "Do nothing from selfish ambition or conceit, but in humility count others more significant than yourselves" (ESV).

I confronted my fear of speaking so that I could be in service. I worked with a voice coach, and speaking became a whole new career.

As I matured, I realized that staying quiet is a form of arrogance. What I'm doing when I stay quiet is protecting my ego from criticism, essentially, making it all about me! I know now that one of the most softhearted things we can do is share what we know. It's a win-win. When we're serving others, we get to feel empowered, and they get to learn from our experiences and our mistakes.

STRENGTH IN CHANGE

After repeatedly being told that no one would listen to me and that I was "just a bimbo," I intentionally built a business that had nothing to do with my looks.

It's a good thing I did, because my sense of adventure often outweighs my sense of grace. One day my husband and I were goofing around in the driveway wagon surfing. I overcorrected a turn and flew into the air, coming down hard face first on the bricks.

When I regained consciousness, Greg, who is always calm, was standing over me with a look of horror on his face—and he was praying.

The healing process was long and painful. My face was badly injured, and we had to pivot several projects, as I was not able to make appearances during that time.

Yet as the dust settled and my team and I regrouped, the data showed that during the time I was invisible, kathy ireland Worldwide had the largest growth spurt in company history.

I felt so grateful. That news was validation that my looks had nothing to do with our success; it was our values, drive, and desire to help others that continued to propel us forward.

When COVID hit, we had to pivot again, and still our business grew. I learned two lessons from these unexpected events. The first was not to fear unexpected change. The second was that it's much smarter to anticipate and initiate change than be forced to react to it.

Philippians 4:6–7 says, "Be anxious for nothing, but in everything by prayer and supplication, with thanksgiving, let your requests be made known to God" (NKJV).

Life is unpredictable. People pass away, jobs are lost, relationships fizzle, and faces get rearranged by brick driveways! It's vital that we all find something to hold on to when it feels like everything is falling apart, something permanent to borrow courage from when life throws us into fear, something to lean in to that can never be taken from us.

For me that something is my faith. With faith, we can navigate, survive, and rise above any change!

Strength in Alignment

As a woman in business, I'm proud that my team and I have defied the notion that success and kindness are mutually exclusive, and we are committed to achieving our goals with empathy and compassion.

Our company serves ten initiatives ranging from alleviating hunger and poverty, to finding cures for diseases, to fighting human trafficking and environmental issues. When we meet with a potential partner, our mission is to help them grow their bottom line, but also to add to our ecosystem of service. If they're not interested in supporting one of the initiatives, either with financial support or volunteer work, we move on. We've walked away from deals that had the potential to generate millions of dollars because the business owner's values did not align with ours.

I've learned that to live a life that feels whole, you've got to know what you value, what you stand for, and whom you can count on to help you in your mission.

In Corinthians, scripture says to "stand firm in the faith; be courageous; be strong" (1 Cor. 16:13, NIV).

I've come to understand that true strength comes from never being a doormat, never succumbing to fear, and never allowing the opinions of others to define you. It comes from intentionally placing the needs of others above your own and making the conscious decision every day to face every challenge and embrace every critic.

Strong people are not fearless; they just resolve to act in the face of fear and to get up no matter how many times they're knocked down. I've learned so many things the hard way. I look at failure as education, and in that respect, I'm very well educated!

In the end, I like to think that kathy ireland Worldwide has proven that success and faith can walk hand in hand, demonstrating that in business, as in life, our greatest strength is our character and our greatest victories are those aligned with our hearts.

About Kathy

Kathy Ireland enjoys a global platform as a result of proven leadership in human rights advocacy, the support of millions of women, as well as families, who embrace Ireland's designs, products, and services, unified under the *kathy ireland*® Worldwide philosophy of empowered living.

Ireland is cofounder of *kathy ireland*® Worldwide, the world's sixteenth-most successful brand according to License Global! and "the most valuable woman-owned licensing company in American history," according to WWD.

By adhering to a mission statement of "Finding solutions for families, especially busy moms," Ireland earns the honor and title of "best friend to working mothers" from both Associated Press and the London Times.

"Super Model turned Super Mogul" is a term *Forbes* coined to describe Ireland, after great success in transitioning from an iconic modeling career to a powerful business tycoon. Ireland's fashion career began on covers including *Teen, Harper's Bazaar, Vogue, Cosmopolitan*, and, of course, *Sports Illustrated*'s best-selling swimsuit cover of all time. As of 2022 Ireland has graced the cover of *Forbes* three times, in celebration of becoming, according to *Forbes*, one of America's most successful self-made women.

UCLA named Ireland "one of the top ten women's health advocates in America today." Ireland has also been presented with an honorary Doctorate of Humane Letters by the California State University, stating Ireland "generously uses her power and influence to benefit others, supporting social causes including empowering women, supporting young girls through mentoring, and providing opportunities for girls and women at risk."

Ireland has graced the cover of *Forbes* magazine as many times as *Sports Illustrated* and is responsible for billions of dollars in retail sales. Ireland is the first female board member of the NFLPI, WNBPA Board of Advocates, and recipient of The International Home Furnishings Representatives Association (IHFRA) highly coveted ICON Award.

On July 15, 2021, Ireland received the inaugural International Religious Freedom Business Champion Award at the IRF Summit in Washington, DC, and has received multiple awards in support of many philanthropic efforts including women's and children's health, HIV/AIDS, education, human freedom, human rights, wars against religious persecution, and anti-violence of every kind. Ireland's advocacy for nonprofits includes honors from, in addition to financial support, services, ambassadorships, or board of director memberships for American European Bethel Mission (AEBM), Dream Foundation, Dream Center Los Angeles, Providence Educational Foundation, and Providence School (cofounder), 911 for Kids/AEFK, Advisory Board for James Madison Program at Princeton University, National PTA, Hardwired Global, National Pediatric Cancer Foundation (international youth chair), American Cancer Society, Arthritis Foundation, Foreseeable Future Foundation, American Society of Gastrointestinal Endoscopy (board member), Elizabeth Taylor AIDS Foundation, WIZO, Jewish National Fund, Free Burma Rangers, Didi Hirsch Mental Health Services, Los Angeles Team Mentoring, and Anne Graham Lotz AnGel Ministries, among others.

CHAPTER 2

THE GIFT OF ADVERSITY

*From Fierce to Fragile: One Woman's
Journey to Reclaiming Her Strength*

By Christie Hensler

As I lay on my cold, hard bedroom floor, I trembled in sheer terror, my heart pounding in my chest, desperately begging God to take me. With my hands shaking uncontrollably, I reached for my husband's handgun, ready to silence this torment forever. But in that moment of darkness a vision blazed before me: I saw myself standing on a stage, facing a sea of people, inspiring them to conquer their own battles.

In the grip of a full-blown panic attack, I made a life-changing decision. I would fight for my sanity, my mental health, and my future. If I could break free from the chains of debilitating OCD, irrational fears, depression, anxiety, panic attacks, and suicidal thoughts, I could light the way for others to slay their own demons. I just needed to keep searching for answers.

How did I transform from a strong, fierce, highly motivated Christian girl with world-changing dreams into a thirty-three-year-old woman barely clinging to life, contemplating suicide? This is the story of how I crumbled and then rebuilt myself.

At first glance, it seemed life suddenly punched me in the face and left me for dead. But looking back, I see a series of trials, choices, and adopted mindsets that gradually led me to this place of isolation and desperation.

At seventeen I lost my best friend to cancer. I had a choice to make on how I would respond to grief and heartache.

At nineteen I married in the church, only to divorce at twenty-five. As a Christian woman, I never imagined myself standing at the divorce podium, facing judgment from those around me. I grappled with how to respond and whether I could extend grace to myself.

Then came a yearlong secret affair with my best friend—both of us still married to others. It was a whirlwind of lies, manipulation, and eventual heartbreak. The disastrous ending landed me in the mental health ward against my will. It took years, even decades, to learn to trust again and forgive myself for the choices I made and the pain I caused myself and others.

In the aftermath of this turmoil, I met Matt, my current husband. We married just months after my affair ended, diving head-first into a relationship neither of us was truly ready for. The first five years of our marriage were nothing short of living hell. I was as broken as a stolen car abandoned in the hood, carrying the weight of my past mistakes and unresolved trauma. Matt, on the other hand, was as naive as they come, unprepared for the storm of emotions and challenges we'd face. We would have divorced had it not been for two pastor couples in our lives who stood by us, offering guidance, support, and a beacon of hope when we could see none ourselves. Looking back, staying together would end up being one of the best decisions of my life. I had no idea of the storms that lay ahead, nor how desperately I would need a loyal, stable, and patient partner like Matt to weather them. His unwavering presence would become my anchor in the tumultuous years to come.

A battle with infertility and other health challenges left me searching for answers beyond conventional medicine, eventually leading me to explore natural health and holistic healing. That experience ultimately led me to birthing all three of my children at home and delivering a miscarried baby at home. This journey through fertility struggles and alternative approaches to healthcare would profoundly shape my perspective on life, health, and personal strength.

By my early thirties I should have been living my dream as a wife, mom, and entrepreneur. Instead, I was trapped in a nightmare. Panic and anxiety attacks left me trembling in corners, paralyzed with fear and unable to care for my children. My husband would return from work to find me in this state. From the moment I opened my eyes until I fell asleep, my brain was plagued with irrational fears. The more I tried to control my OCD and intrusive thoughts, the more they controlled me. Even simple tasks like showering would leave me collapsed, hyperventilating, and shaking uncontrollably.

Desperate for solutions beyond medication, we invested years and thousands of dollars trying various treatments, therapies, and supplements. Some offered a glimmer of hope, while others seemed futile.

One morning, as Matt prepared for work, I begged him to stay home. Despite my pleas, he left, knowing he had to provide for our family. Paralyzed by fear, I spent eight hours in the sun, heavily pregnant, while our toddlers played. Matt returned to find me with second-degree burns, unable to walk or put any clothes on. For a week, he carried me everywhere.

After that incident, I couldn't be alone. My mom stepped in to help daily, but the mental torment persisted. Pregnant with our third child, I even considered adoption, feeling incapable of caring for another baby. Matt's unwavering support kept us going, but after seven years of struggle, hope was fading. Only the vision of helping others kept me fighting.

By November 2014 I was getting extremely weary and losing the fight. We knew drastic change was necessary. We made the gut-wrenching decision and took out a home equity loan, and Matt quit his dream job to be with me full time. We didn't realize then that rebuilding our financial security would take a decade.

Miraculously, in February 2015 the right supplements helped

my body and mind begin to heal. Sometimes our miracles in life come in ways we least expect.

Seeking a fresh start, we sold everything, bought an old RV, and hit the road. What was meant to be a six-month adventure turned into eighteen months of trials and unexpected breakdowns across the country.

Our journey evolved into living in fully furnished Airbnbs, with all our belongings fitting in our car trunk. In January 2023, after eight years of nomadic life, we finally set down roots. While not always glamorous, this journey was integral to my healing.

This past decade has been about undoing harmful mindsets, breaking patterns of fear, and becoming a healthier version of myself. It's been my life's greatest challenge, but I'm grateful for the progress and where I stand today. My journey isn't over—I'm still learning, growing, and healing every day. I haven't "arrived" at perfection, nor do I expect to, but I've come to embrace the ongoing process of personal growth.

Life often leads us down unexpected paths, some fraught with challenges we never anticipated. At nineteen, brimming with dreams and ambitions, I couldn't have foreseen the adversity that awaited me. Yet after twenty-five years of navigating life's twists and turns, I've come to recognize adversity as one of my greatest gifts.

Embracing adversity has the power to transform your life in ways you might never imagine. It can unlock the deeper fulfillment you crave and propel you towards becoming the best version of yourself. Here's how adversity has shaped me:

- It's forged a hard-fought wisdom and depth of character that now guides me through life's challenges.

- It's cultivated genuine empathy and humility inside of me, replacing judgment with compassion and grace. It wasn't always that way.

- It's taught me to find joy in the journey and appreciate life's simple pleasures.

- It's built an unshakable confidence born from resilience, freeing me to pursue my dreams without fear knowing I'm equipped to handle whatever life throws my way.

- It's deepened my faith and trust in God, becoming a cornerstone of my journey and a source of unwavering strength.

- It's freed me from the calculated version of myself I'd become, allowing me to discover and embrace who I was truly created to be, unlocking my authentic self and fullest potential.

These aren't just personal anecdotes; they're universal truths waiting to be discovered. The adversity you face right now could be the key to unlocking a more fulfilling, authentic, and powerful version of yourself. It's not about seeking out hardship, but about harnessing the challenges life inevitably brings to fuel your growth and transformation.

Are you ready to reframe your adversity as an opportunity? To tap into the strength you never knew you had? To emerge from your challenges not just stronger, but wiser, more compassionate, and more alive? The tools to do so are within your reach, and I'm here to share them with you so you don't have to spend years searching for them, as I did.

SELF-AWARENESS

"Knowing yourself is the beginning of all wisdom."
—ARISTOTLE

Imagine having a superpower that guides you through life's storms with clarity and purpose. That's what self-awareness offers when facing adversity.

When challenges arise, we're often flooded with emotions and stress. But understanding yourself deeply equips you to navigate these turbulent waters. Knowing your triggers, fears, joys, and core values provides instant clarity on what's causing your stress and emotional reactions.

Without self-awareness, we're like ships without rudders, tossed about by circumstance. With it, you can pause, reflect, and respond intentionally. You're no longer just reacting emotionally; you're making conscious choices aligned with your true self.

John Maxwell said, "Reflection turns experience into insight." By regularly reflecting on your experiences, you transform raw events into valuable life lessons. Set aside time daily for self-reflection, ask yourself tough questions, and be brutally honest with your answers.

Try these powerful questions to boost your self-awareness:

- What situations consistently trigger strong emotions in me, and why?

- What are my nonnegotiable values, and how do they influence my decisions?

- What brings me genuine joy and fulfillment?

As you cultivate self-awareness, you'll be better equipped to identify root causes of stress, make aligned decisions, communicate effectively, and recognize areas for growth.

Self-awareness is a journey, not a destination. Be patient with yourself, celebrate your insights, and keep exploring your inner world.

PERSPECTIVE

"Your perspective will either become your prison or your passport."

—STEVEN FURTICK

We all have a choice: to be a victim or a victor. We can view life's challenges as happening *to* us, leaving us bitter and resentful, or *for* us, allowing us to grow and evolve. The power of the right mindset determines whether we merely survive adversity or thrive through it.

My journey through debilitating mental health issues robbed me of precious memories from my children's early years. There are no family photos, just a blur of survival. I could dwell on all that was lost—time, memories, money, opportunities, relationships. Instead, I choose to focus on who I've become through this adversity. This perspective has transformed me into a more present wife, mother, and coach, with heightened emotional intelligence and empathy that allows me to empower my children and others on their journeys.

Remember, you have the power to choose your perspective in any situation. If you struggle to find the right viewpoint, don't hesitate to seek help from others. Sometimes, when you're in the frame, it's hard to see the whole picture clearly.

To help shift your perspective, consider these powerful questions:

- Is this a temporary inconvenience or a life-altering crisis?

- Am I looking at this challenge through a lens of a healthy perspective?

- A year from now, how will I view this current struggle differently?

Before you go any further into your situation, stop and choose your perspective.

EMBRACE PAIN

Sometimes the only way out is through. In a world that often encourages escaping discomfort, true growth comes from facing our challenges head-on. Early in my journey, I sought to bypass the pain of heartbreak and failed relationships by rushing into new ones or burying myself in work. This only led to more suffering and delayed my necessary personal growth.

Society offers countless distractions from our difficulties—food, the internet, alcohol, gambling, pornography, and excessive work, just to name a few. But by running from our "hard," we miss the transformative power waiting on the other side. Had I given up on my second marriage when things were tough, and believe me they were, I would have lost the chance to build an enviable relationship with an incredible partner. Our bond today is a testament to embracing pain, choosing growth, and maintaining unwavering commitment against all odds.

One caution: It's crucial to distinguish between toxic situations and opportunities for growth. Once you identify a chance for personal development, resist the urge to escape. Instead, ask yourself:

- How can this adversity make me stronger?
- What would my best self do in this situation?
- What hidden opportunity lies within this challenge?

By leaning in to discomfort and seeking its lessons, you open the door to profound personal transformation and a richer, more fulfilling life.

SUPPORT SYSTEM

Embrace your lifeline through adversity. As a fiercely independent woman, I never imagined how crucial a support system would be. Yet I owe my life to my husband, Matt, and our marriage's survival to two influential couples who guided us through our early years.

A strong support system is critical, but remember: it's about quality, not quantity. You need the right support. Just as you wouldn't trust a 385-pound couch potato as a fitness coach or a four-time divorcee as a marriage counselor, your support system should consist of people who've overcome similar challenges.

Seek out those who've been where you are and have made it to the other side. Additionally, consider including someone who thinks differently from you, with complementary personality and strengths. For me that's Matt. He wasn't what I thought I wanted in a husband, but he was everything I needed—my rock, whose loyalty, commitment, and belief in me have been instrumental in my journey.

Questions to ask yourself when looking for the right support:

- Who are the people in my life that consistently lift me up and push me to grow?

- What gaps exist in my current support system, and how can I fill them?

- How can I be a better support for others while also nurturing my own growth?

Be willing to invest your time, energy, and resources into getting the right support—your future may just depend on it. Some of the most valuable people in my life have been life and business coaches.

Friend, whatever challenges you're facing right now, remember this: Your current circumstances don't define your future.

Rewind to that pivotal day: Trembling on my bedroom floor, I had a vision of standing on a stage, inspiring others. Today, I'm living that vision, transforming my deepest struggles into a message of hope.

You have a unique purpose in this world. Every struggle you've endured or are enduring can become a source of strength. These experiences, painful as they may be, can empower you to reach your full potential, find deep fulfillment, and discover genuine joy in your journey. Your adversities aren't roadblocks; they're stepping stones to a more resilient, confident, and purposeful you. I'm right there with you cheering you on, while running my own race!

About Christie

Christie never wanted a normal life. Ever. From a young age her focus was on leading people and making a significant impact in the world, undeterred by others' expectations of degrees, stable jobs, or opinions on how her life should unfold. Her journey has been extraordinary, filled with adversity, setbacks, and opportunities disguised as great challenges.

After a long and arduous mental health battle, Christie and her family made the bold decision to sell everything they owned, purchase an old RV, and embark on a life-changing journey across the United States. This unexpected experience allowed them to rebuild their lives from the ground up, start a thriving business, and impact countless individuals along the way.

In her powerful book, *Life Hacks for Hard Times*, Christie shares the transformative tools and strategies that helped her navigate life's toughest challenges and emerge stronger and better than ever. Her raw vulnerability and hard-won wisdom offer readers a lifeline during their own darkest moments, inspiring them to persevere.

As a dynamic speaker, certified coach, and DISC consultant, Christie engages audiences with passion, creating an interactive and immersive experience that leaves a lasting impact. With her keen insights, she provides clients with the clarity they need to overcome obstacles and create a clear path forward.

Christie values authenticity over accolades and hype. She cherishes real connections and genuine moments, with a knack for making people laugh and a lighthearted approach to life that reminds us all not to take ourselves too seriously. Christie is married to her best friend, Matt, and together they are raising three daughters, equipping them with the tools to handle life's curveballs and live intentionally.

In *Strength*, Christie invites readers to embrace adversity as an unexpected but necessary gift, a catalyst for personal growth and transformation. Her mission is to empower individuals and organizations to unlock their full potential and live each day with purpose, proving that a life of true fulfillment is within everyone's reach, regardless of the challenges they face.

When not inspiring others through her writing, speaking, or coaching,

Christie can be found tending to her houseplants or exploring new coffee and pottery shops. While she might fall asleep within minutes of any movie, a football game captivates her for hours.

Christie's life motto is simple yet profound: Be competent. Be consistent. Be courageous.

Connect with her at www.christiehensler.com and on LinkedIn at www.linkedin.com/in/christiehensler.

CHAPTER 3

THE POWER OF BELIEF

Overcoming Mental Obstacles to
Unlock Your True Potential

By Tiffany Whitney

I t's the kind of phone call every mother dreads.

The kind that creates a definitive line in the sand designating a life divided into two parts: before and after.

My ex-husband's voice sounded strained and exhausted, and his words sent a chill down my spine, producing in me a cocktail blend of emotions ranging from worry to rage to absolute dread.

He'd been out of the country with our son when something went terribly wrong. My son, it seems, was suffering from a mental health crisis. His father had dropped him off at a rehabilitation center in Florida and threw me the ball.

I'd have to get there, fast, and figure out what was happening to my son.

Memories of my boy from infant to a now grown man moved like a carousel through my mind. I threw what I could into a suitcase and booked the flight, my only goal to get to my son as soon as possible.

I was in no way prepared for what I would find when I got there. My son, the bright young man I had known, was nowhere to be found. Whatever was happening to him had rendered him panicked and incapacitated with little grasp on reality.

Over the next few years, my husband and I cared for him day and night. We couldn't leave him alone for a minute. The doctors suggested we give up, throw in the towel and accept the fact that our only hope was finding him a place at an institution.

Give up?

Giving up was not in my vocabulary. There was no way I was going to let my smart, beautiful son waste away in some sterile building. Not when I could still see a spark of his old self behind his eyes.

Something clicked in me that day. A fierce determination reawakened, and I made up my mind to learn everything I could about how the brain works, why we think how we think, and the human body's inherent capacity for healing and regeneration.

It paid off.

Today, my son is a different person. He has good friends and drives himself to work and social gatherings. He is funny and engaging and lives as close to a normal life as possible.

If I had listened to the doctors, he'd be dead.

I can't tell you how many times in my life the evidence suggested I should just give up.

Have you been there?

You're hitting roadblock after roadblock, getting knocked down again and again, and then it happens.

Your mind starts presenting you with all the reasons you just can't, and won't ever, get ahead. All the labels, the insults, and the criticism you've ever heard rise to the top of your mind. Suddenly, it doesn't matter how capable you are or how much you've already achieved; those limiting beliefs scream louder and louder!

When I dove headfirst into the study of neuroscience, I realized that I'd been using the principles of it for years in my corporate work.

I started my job in 1985 and steadily moved up the ladder from typist to assistant to the head of a branch to director of multiple offices to leading the talent development for a global company.

I was respected, leading teams, and living what most people would call a very successful life.

No one was more surprised by that than me.

You see, I never thought I was smart enough to work in a corporate setting because I didn't have a degree. Then, I thought I could never reach the level of success I wanted to because I was a single mom of two kids. Then, I told myself there was no way I could *sustain* any kind of success because I have an autoimmune disease that sometimes makes it hard to function.

Why do we do this to ourselves?

Why is our default setting so relentlessly self-sabotaging?

And how do we stop that train of sabotaging thoughts and reach our full potential?

When my son was ill, I learned so much about neuroplasticity and how we can rewire our brains to function in a way that serves us. Imagine that! No matter what you're going through, there's a chance you can train your brain to form new neural pathways that actually help you heal and grow.

Today, I'm a Career Ownership Coach®, and my job is to use my experience in neuroscientific practices to help my clients overcome their limiting beliefs, dial into a more productive and fulfilling way of being, and ultimately create the exact life they want to live.

It's possible for anyone.

You've just got to learn how to garden.

Pruning the Dead Leaves

Gardening is a cyclical dance between seeding, nurturing, and pruning away any part of the plant hindering the growth.

I'm an avid gardener, and as I water and prune each day, I'm reminded of the parallels it holds to how we must care for our minds. We've got to cultivate a practice of checking on our mental garden and removing the invasive weeds that are choking the life out of the parts of us that could otherwise bloom.

Your limiting beliefs are like out-of-control vines, strangling your spirit.

That's why the process of introspection is so important. Vines grow fast! As do negative thoughts and self-criticism. You've got to constantly keep an eye on what you're allowing to grow, weeds or flowers.

Negative, limiting thoughts, or positive, productive ones?

It's entirely possible for you to change your life no matter how deep the roots of your belief system run.

You do this by first identifying the limiting belief, and then questioning and examining the evidence.

You can challenge the validity of the belief by asking yourself tough questions, the most important being this: "Is there any real evidence to support the belief *today*, or is it based on a past experience?"

For the longest time I fought unexplained symptoms that exhausted my body and strained my mental outlook. Doctors treated me for everything from Hashimoto's disease to chronic fatigue syndrome to rheumatoid arthritis, but nothing helped.

If you've ever worked in a competitive corporate environment, you'll understand my desire to keep my illness hidden.

Corporate leaders need workers and winners. They spare no time for people who need more time off than others. If you even hint at health issues, you'll be passed up for a younger version of yourself. You've got to keep up. When the team goes out to celebrate, you've got to show your face. If you don't, you'll get overlooked and left behind.

At least that's what my limiting beliefs were telling me. For twenty years I hid my health struggle, convinced it would be the death of my career.

Over time I earned the trust and respect of my bosses and colleagues. I'd been tasked with teaching employees how to perform different roles in the insurance industry. I was doing so well that I developed an entire training program. The program was so successful that other branches across the country asked if they could use it. I created an entirely new division within our company and grew it from training just a few employees in our branch to training twenty-seven thousand employees and customers nationwide each year.

The best part was I could run this division from home, allowing me to manage my symptoms without any disruption in work.

All those years, I had told myself that I could never be successful due to my health, but that was never a *fact*. The fact was that I had symptoms to manage. All the other stories I was telling myself were beliefs I'd totally made up.

The evidence showed that not only could I function, but I could also be wildly successful on my own terms despite my health challenges.

If you're going through anything you think you can't handle, if you want something, and you think it's impossible, question the evidence. Liberate yourself from those wild, fictional tales so the truth can bring its gifts.

REFRAMING THE NARRATIVE

"He's out to get me," my client said, his face tense, his hand slapping the desk. "He doesn't like me, and he's trying to sabotage me!"

Scott had just started coming to see me, and over the past couple of weeks, I had noticed he was increasingly frustrated with his boss. The stories were compounding. He told me that the boss was contacting his team without notifying him first or copying him in the emails.

It was obvious that the boss was trying to devalue my client's authority and turn the team's loyalty to himself.

Or was he?

After getting to know each other, my client realized that the boss wasn't undermining him at all. The boss was simply very people-oriented and saw it as his duty to communicate with employees at all levels.

My client had wasted months feeling stressed and angry, all because he had concocted a story, adopted it as truth, and let it control his experience. The boss had never said a mean word to him. He hadn't heard any rumors that the boss disliked him. All his negativity was fiction, and he was the author!

Now, with the narrative reframed, he was enjoying his job, had forged a great relationship with his boss, and was looking forward to a long career with the company.

When something is bothering you, ask yourself if you can be 100 percent certain that what you believe is true.

If you have no hard evidence, let go of the story that's sabotaging you and allow for one that serves you.

MASTER THE ART OF VISION

Once you've identified a limiting belief, examined the evidence, and realized that it was all in your mind, it's time to master the art of creating a preferred vision.

A Pinterest vision board isn't going to cut it.

The key is to be specific and reach high!

When I ask my clients what they want and they say they want to make a ton of money, I send them back to the drawing board.

A guy who used to work on my team came to me for coaching. He wanted to start a business but didn't believe he'd be successful due to some health challenges that prevented him from being highly visible and outgoing.

I encouraged him to construct his ideal day down to the hour. I asked him to write down exactly what he would do each hour if he knew that it would be profitable to do it *his* own way.

He realized he could in fact offer a highly valued service that allowed him to work independently and from home and launched a very successful bookkeeping practice.

Get granular!

If there is something you want to change, envision the absolute best-case scenario. Not the one you think is possible based on false evidence. Not the one you would settle for but the version of reality that would make you truly happy. Then map out by the day, by the hour, what it would look like to live in this vision.

This is not daydreaming.

There is scientific proof that consistently imagining yourself doing something changes the neural networks in your brain.

Have you ever heard a story about someone being told they would never walk again and yet a few months later they are walking just fine? That's the magic of neuroplasticity.

And the best part is you don't need a medical degree to make it happen.

Give yourself permission to visualize the outcome you want, and allow yourself to get lost in that vision as often as you can. You are training your brain for change and success!

Take Action

"I'm unreachable, and I'm not going to send you any more money."

I couldn't believe it. My ex-husband disappeared out of the country, and he was no longer going to pay child support.

I was stunned.

I'd been living with my two young children in Nevada, but I hated it. So a few months before that call, I had taken action. I mustered up the courage to pack up my kids and everything we owned and move to Arizona. I wanted my degree. So I took more action and applied to attend Arizona State University. I had saved enough money to buy a condo and planned to use the child support and alimony to finally graduate from college.

Now, just two months in, my plan was in shambles. There was no way I could afford to go to school and pay for childcare without his help. I would need to find a job as soon as possible.

I was devastated, of course, but had learned that the fastest way out of discomfort was, you guessed it, *action*!

I'd worked in the insurance industry before. In fact, it was the only industry I knew, so with resume in hand, I marched into every title insurance office I could find in downtown Phoenix.

I didn't drop my resume off. I sat in every lobby, sometimes for hours, until a manager would speak with me.

It worked.

I got a job, climbed the corporate ladder, built a hugely rewarding career, and then, when management changed and the business model no longer aligned with my values, I took action *again* to start my own company as a career coach.

Action is the antidote to limiting beliefs. It's through action that we gather new bodies of evidence to support better, more empowering narratives.

Action waters new beliefs into being. And once those new beliefs take root, the weeds of your past experiences, assumptions, and stories can be buried once and for all!

TAKE THE REINS

Imagine that you're driving down a highway and the traffic is terrible, the construction is messy and awful, and the road is flooded with mud, debris, and dangerous obstacles.

Your GPS suggests that you take the next exit and detour through a less treacherous route.

That's what's possible in your brain.

There is great strength in self-examination. Without it your thoughts continue on the dark and dangerous highway.

With it, however, your neurons can travel a new route, splitting off and forming new pathways toward better, healthier results.

As I reflect on my journey, I can't help but marvel at the transformative power of self-examination and redirection.

Each time I faced a daunting highway in life, I rerouted my thoughts and remembered my mother's belief that I could do absolutely anything if only I believed it.

And so can you.

You simply have to write better stories for yourself. As soon as a limiting belief comes knocking, throw it out as total fiction and focus on this truth: You are the author. You are the driver. You decide the route and the destination.

And you, against all odds, can train your brain to create a rich and fulfilling life as the best, strongest, and happiest version of yourself.

About Tiffany

Tiffany Whitney's story is about ambition, expertise, and a heartfelt commitment to transforming lives and careers. With over twenty years' experience in the learning and development arena of a Fortune 500 company, Tiffany has dedicated her career to facilitating growth for individuals and organizations.

As a Career Ownership Coach at The Entrepreneur's Source and CEO of Feed Your Brain LLC, Tiffany empowers professionals to take control of their careers. Her approach goes beyond finding the next job; it's about understanding one's behaviors and motivations, leveraging innate strengths, and taking career ownership that aligns with aspirations and values.

During her tenure as senior director of Learning and Business Implementation at First American Title Insurance Co., Tiffany led groundbreaking initiatives that have left a lasting impact on the industry. She spearheaded the national rollouts of TRID, ALTA Best Practices, and Remote Online Notary (RON), touching 27,000 employees and customers and managing a multimillion-dollar budget. Her leadership and innovation spearheading the largest learning and development programs in the title insurance industry inspire others to push boundaries and make a difference.

Tiffany's unique approach blends scientific insights with practical application, underpinned by her credentials, which include a Certificate in the Foundations of Neuroleadership and a Brain-Based Coaching Certificate. This method has revolutionized the way individuals approach their professional growth.

Beyond her professional achievements, Tiffany's interests in public speaking and learning architecture reflect her passion for communication and structured growth. Her unwavering belief in every individual's potential to shape their destiny is a testament to her core values. This belief instills a sense of empowerment and hope in those she works with, inspiring them to reach their highest potential.

Tiffany is a beacon for professionals feeling stuck or uncertain, illuminating a path forward with clarity and confidence. She is not just a coach but a guide, mentor, and innovator, transforming the career development landscape with every life she touches.

Connecting with Tiffany is an invitation to explore your potential, redefine your objectives, and embark on professional and personal fulfillment. Step into a future where your career is not just a job but a reflection of your deepest values and aspirations.

Contact Tiffany:

www.tiffanywhitney.coach

www.linkedin.com/in/tiffanywhitney

CHAPTER 4

MISSION POSSIBLE

By Larry Kozin

A s I slowly emerged from the blackness of unconsciousness, a heavy sensation set in.

My body felt weak and sluggish, as if each movement required an unfathomable effort. I squinted my eyes from the glaring light above me, trying to piece together where I was and how I got there.

It didn't take long for fragments of memories to flash across my mind. Clinking glasses, roaring laughter, and blurred faces danced around my brain. I didn't remember much else, but a painful realization was settling in. The love of my life, Angie, who was in Mexico with me, had walked away from me because of my stupor.

The guilt and shame were suffocating as the truth took hold. I had once again succumbed to my addiction. I hadn't told her that I was an alcoholic. One thing addicts are great at, at least in the beginning, is hiding our demons.

I hadn't even admitted to myself that I was an alcoholic. Alcoholics in my mind were people that drank vodka for breakfast and couldn't show up for work. I didn't fit that description, so I tricked myself into believing I had it all under control.

I can't imagine how shocking it must have been for her to watch me binge and black out. I knew in that moment that the lifelong relationship I'd always wanted was about to disappear, as well as my dreams of being a good father and an entrepreneur with enough success to empower and help other people.

I come by all this dysfunction honestly.

As a child, my parents divorced, and I processed that trauma by developing a collection of unhealthy habits, the worst of which was alcohol.

Years before, the health care plan I was applying for required a routine doctor's visit. I expected the doctor to give me a clean bill of health and send me on my way. Instead, he delivered a shocking blow. After years of abusing my own body, I was diagnosed with liver disease, which at the time had no cure and was often fatal.

I would love to say that the news prompted me to change my life. But that's not what happened.

I didn't see the diagnosis as an opportunity to change, but rather as a solid reason to give up.

I sank further into depression, managing my sadness with more alcohol. What did it matter? I was going to die anyway. It was that line of thought that led to me being blacked out in Mexico.

After that day, I finally realized that I couldn't take another chance on destroying my career or damaging my relationships with my children and the woman who is, thankfully, now my wife. That was eighteen years ago, and your bottom will hopefully not be as desperate and desolate as mine. But if it is, or even worse, the great news is this: With each new day, we are given an opportunity to find the strength to dream fearlessly and start over.

Today, I am the founder, chairman, and CEO of MainStreetChamber Holdings (U.S. OTC—MSCH), as well as cofounder of kathy ireland Licensing. Our companies have holdings all over the globe, and our mission is to help independent companies expand internationally and give them an opportunity to be part of a growing family of holdings.

Today I travel all over the world and am living a life of abundance and joy. It's a far cry from being broke and passed out drunk in a Mexican alley.

I have a deep spirituality to thank for this life I get to live. What I've realized over the years is that the same principles I relied on to pull me back from the brink of addiction and into a life of meaning are very much applicable to the world of business and to building success.

They are principles of integrity, character, honoring your word, serving others, and surrendering to the flow of things with total faith that there's a gift in every circumstance and a lesson that will lead you straight to your most fulfilling life.

You don't have to be a recovering addict to benefit from that kind of advice. In fact, if everyone lived by these principles, this world would be a much healthier, happier, and more abundant place.

BUILD CONNECTIONS, NOT TRANSACTIONS

One of the most important cornerstones of success is the relationships you form and nurture.

Human beings are wired for partnership and community. We are not meant to go it alone. In fact, years ago, going it alone meant certain death! We needed our tribe to protect us, feed us, and provide for us an identity we could hold on to. The idea that there is strength in numbers still holds true in life and in business.

The saying "Your network is your net worth" is a testament to the importance of operating with integrity and forging powerful bonds.

In 2022 I was running a very successful licensing and furniture business and was in the process of going public. Thanks to some great relationships I had developed, I had the chance to meet Stephen Roseberry, the president of kathy ireland Worldwide, at a licensing show. Kathy is a powerhouse who has now been on the cover of *Forbes* magazine more times than she's been on the cover of *Sports Illustrated*! I was thrilled to learn that she was interested in partnering with us in our children's furniture business, and we negotiated a licensing contract. It was the largest contract I had ever signed, and I was ecstatic over this partnership.

However, things did not go as planned. We were not able to have the prototypes developed within the time frames we had estimated, and other supply chain issues were in play due to world events beyond our control. We had no clause for random, unprecedented events, so we were still responsible for the payment obligations to kiWW.

I was stuck in an endless inner debate that was getting me nowhere. Should I default? Declare bankruptcy? Fake my own death and move to another country?

In the end I banked on the strength of the relationships I had built and the trust I had cultivated with my colleagues. I approached Kathy's team with total honesty and a few options. I took my story to Kathy and Stephen, who presented it to their board of directors, and they liked what I had proposed as a solution. The culmination of those conversations was an amazing partnership with Kathy's company. In a move that hadn't been done in more than thirty-five years, we became equity owners in their brand, and they became the largest shareholder in our public company, which had just started trading on OTC.

Build relationships, nurture those relationships, and turn to them when life throws a wrench in your plans.

There is great strength in honesty and vulnerability.

When you can bring yourself to ask for help, you might get more than you could ever have imagined.

Take Inventory, Even When It Hurts

One of the most important lessons I've learned both in business and in life is to take inventory, admit wrongdoings, and strive to replace any character defect with a new and better value.

When I first started my career in furniture sales, I got some bad advice.

And I followed it.

My mentors at that time were cutthroat salesmen willing to say whatever they needed to say to close a sale, regardless of whether it was true or in the customer's best interest.

They had metrics to meet and would meet them at any cost. I followed suit.

It turns out, karma is a real thing. While I hit some great goals in the beginning, it didn't take long for it all to unravel.

Through my recovery journey I developed a deep spirituality that prompted me to completely change my ways. I made up my mind that I would grow with integrity, or I wouldn't grow at all.

Taking a moral and financial inventory requires you to determine your values and then regularly assess if the relationships you're in and the decisions you make align with those values.

It's not a one-time thing, but a practice that serves as a compass, pointing the way to intentional choices and strong character.

It actually makes life and business fairly simple. Anytime you have to make a decision, you just return to your inventory of values. Every decision either supports or contradicts those values. You now have a decision-making framework you can turn to at a moment's notice, use as a barometer for life's choices, and know with certainty that you are on the right track.

I made up my mind a long time ago to operate my life and career with the spiritual principles of kindness, generosity, honesty and humility, even if doing so meant taking the long way around.

Sometimes business negotiations can become litigious. I am very proud to say that in the past eighteen years of working in licensing with my business partner John Bellave, we haven't had a single lawsuit filed against us and have determined not to sue others. We also know that as we grow, we can protect ourselves from the greed we find pervasive on Wall Street.

Even if you did an exhaustive search on the internet, which has become the world's largest bathroom wall on which anyone can anonymously write anything, you won't find any smoking guns. Our online presence is solid, and that is vitally important to us.

When I was in the throes of addiction, my reputation was less than stellar. I was arrogant, I cut corners, and I even did some things I'm not proud of and had to make amends for, but cleaning up the wreckage of my past was necessary in the recovery process.

Today my word is impeccable. It's funny, when I chart the trajectory of my wealth, I can clearly see how the growth of my bank account was directly proportional to the growth of my character.

"Leadership is service, not position."

—TIM FARGO

I used to think that success was measured only by how much money you had in the bank and how many people called you "boss."

But once I started my journey to growth and healing, I learned that true success is not defined by dollars and status but by the ripple effect of impact I could create through helping other people achieve their goals.

Imagine that thousands of business owners are enjoying a life of abundance that can ultimately be traced back to doing business with me. I am deeply moved by the thought of that fact, and it propels me to keep living out my purpose year after year.

None of that would be true had I not committed to living by a value system I could be proud of, and that has been proven successful by thousands of recovering addicts who came before me and mentored me. Not just in my personal life, and not just when it was convenient.

But everywhere, always, and with an unwavering commitment to helping others.

When you actively look for ways to give, whether through mentorship, volunteering, or solving problems with new products and services, you unlock a wellspring of inner strength. You prove to yourself that you always have the choice and ability to make a positive impact in the world.

Business does not have to be cutthroat and competitive.

In fact, once I shifted to creating a business based on universal principles of service, kindness, and honesty, my success skyrocketed.

Having been the underdog for years, my partners and I now fight for the underdogs, paying forward the wisdom we've gained over the decades and practicing business in a way that helps people live happy lives of personal, professional, and financial success.

My commitment to living a life rooted in integrity is a strong barometer for me to turn to anytime life or work gets tough. It's a foundation that reminds me of my values and always steers me back on course.

Now, when I am wrong, I promptly admit it and make amends.

When things get tough, I surrender, knowing that a Higher Power will be there for me, and things will always work out exactly as they are supposed to.

When I have a big decision to make, I use prayer and meditation to search for God's will for me and the power to carry it out.

If you are navigating any kind of change that requires you to find an inner strength that you're not sure you have, remembering even just a few of these principles and applying them to all areas of your life can carry you through:

1. Live by a set of values you can be proud of.

2. Act with integrity.

3. Deepen your spiritual practice so you have a safe harbor to rest in when life lands you in uncharted territory.

4. Focus your attention on helping others, as doing so will inevitably help you too.

DESTINY BY CHANCE OR BY CHOICE

I've owed hundreds of thousands of dollars at times and had no assets.

I've been homeless, sleeping at the Salvation Army.

I'm a recovering alcoholic and addict.

I share these things openly because my hope is that my journey gives you the courage to take one of your own.

True strength and success don't come from escaping life but from confronting it head-on.

I used to tell a false and pathetic story to anyone who would listen.

I'm just not cut out to be happy.

I'm just not cut out to be successful.

Thankfully, after having gone through recovery, I tell a very different story now.

Now I know that anything is possible because change simply requires us to cultivate a new set of skills.

Whether you're overcoming addiction, repairing a marriage, or starting a business, there are skills you can learn and sequential steps you can take that lead to the exact outcomes you desire.

Against all odds, and regardless of your past, your fear, and other people's opinions, you can overcome your own limitations, banish self-doubt, and achieve your full potential.

Years ago, under the Mexican sun, I hit rock bottom.

Now I sit here in our beautiful home in paradise, eighteen years sober, with the love of my life. I have built a wildly successful career alongside people I respect and admire, have written best-selling books, and am passionately excited about the projects I'm working on.

I'M HERE BECAUSE I CHOSE TO BE HERE AND RECEIVED THE HELP I NEEDED.

Whatever you're going through, you have a choice. To get the help, to take the steps, to build a vision of hope and happiness and measure every decision against that vision.

I won't tell you it's easy, but I can tell you for sure, with my wife and my cat by my side and the sun on my face, that it's worth it.

About Larry

Larry Kozin is celebrated for his altruistic approach to business, encapsulated by his philosophy to "give first without expecting anything in return." As the founder and CEO of the public company MainStreetChamber Holdings, he is the strategic visionary responsible for their alliance with kathy ireland® Worldwide, the number one female-owned licensing brand in American history.

Larry's pioneering licensing ventures such as iDealFurniture, ireland pay and Aloha Laundry have redefined expansion models. His strategy emphasizes the importance of new economy marketing systems for support and empowerment, crucial for the next generation of entrepreneurs. His steadfast commitment to social causes, particularly child abuse prevention, underscores a corporate ethos that extends beyond commerce, promoting robust community support on a national scale.

Larry's companies have made the Inc. 5000 list three times in the past six years.

Through his extensive business involvements and practical application of his life experiences and skills, Larry has built sales teams numbering in the thousands. He is also the inventor of the world's first furniture vending machine, KozyVEND, which has recently rebranded as kathy ireland Virtual Mall.

Larry currently resides in Las Vegas, Nevada, with his soulmate, Angie, and treasures time spent with his amazing grandkids, Stella, Kane, and Kobe. His authorial endeavors, including coauthoring the best-selling books *Cracking the Code to Success* with sales expert Brian Tracy, as well as *Never Give Up!* with Dickie Vitale, reflect his inspirational journey and solidify his mission to empower entrepreneurs and to overcome life's challenges.

Larry Kozin continues to inspire the integration of business acumen with strong community values, positioning him as a paragon of modern business leadership.

Contact Larry:
Email: LarryKozin@gmail.com
LinkedIn: Larry Kozin
Twitter: @millionairZclub

Website: MSCH.com

CHAPTER 5

CHASING SILVER LININGS

How to Be Great in the Face of Adversity

By Bryan Gallinger

"Something isn't right."

I tried again to lift what should have been an easy amount of weight, only to feel weak and lethargic.

"I probably just need a good night's sleep."

But the next day, after a solid ten hours, I was exhausted, and that night while speaking to four thousand people on stage, I kept cramping up.

Something was happening to me.

Over the next few months, I noticed I was gaining weight at a rapid pace. During my college years, I was an underwear and fitness model and a TV host. Being nice to look at was part of the job requirement, so this sudden onset of extra pounds and the dark circles under my eyes were, in my mind and my agent's, totally unacceptable.

What happened over the next year unfolded like a bad dream.

After months of tests, I learned that my endocrine system was failing. My thyroid had completely shut down. While I could manage some symptoms with medicine, my days of wearing nothing but underwear on a billboard were over.

It was devastating. My whole life I dreamed of being popular and successful. I wanted to be the guy that *other* guys emulated, and girls wanted to date. I was the exact opposite of that until my senior year of high school. In my junior year of high school, my family moved from a small town to a bigger city. I had more kids in my graduating class than in my entire high school back home. Luckily one of the teachers took me under his wing. Under his guidance, I excelled in music and overcame my shyness. I hit the gym twice a day and listened to every personal development course I could get my hands on.

After high school, I started a dream career, touring with bands, competing as a professional athlete, modeling, producing music, hosting TV shows, and living in a house on a lake. As a kid from a small town who had dreamed of working in Hollywood, I was living the life I had envisioned only to watch it come to a screeching halt.

It's a tricky thing when fate takes from you the things by which you've defined yourself. I didn't realize how tightly I'd tied my identity to my career and appearance until both were stripped away.

It wasn't long before the money dried up, my girlfriend left, I gained one hundred pounds and depression set in. You've probably seen enough predictable movies to know what happened next. I coped by developing bad habits and drinking alcohol which, as the cliché goes, led to even more weight gain and worsening depression.

Life had humbled me in a dramatic way, but luckily, the seeds of mindset work had already been planted. At my lowest, the words of great mentors like Tony Robbins and John Maxwell played in my mind, pulled me out of the abyss, and landed me in the middle of my destiny.

In that defining moment, I chose to focus on what mattered to my soul.

I can tell you from experience that everything *does* happen for a reason. That collision with adversity forced me to know myself in a way I'd never tried to. It opened the door to my true purpose, one that God had always intended but that I might not have found had my journey not been interrupted.

Today, I own multiple companies, but my focus is on social impact and humanitarian work. I started exploring ways I could leverage my skills and background to earn a living while making a positive difference in this world. I created Be Great!, a social impact production company. I really wanted to spotlight the people, events and organizations advancing humanity and empowering the planet. By teaming up with some incredible like-minded and like-hearted people, the Be Great! network has helped raise over $50 million for different social causes and organizations.

There are so many exceptional people doing great things in the world, but their effort often goes unrecognized. Be Great! exists to make social impact sexy and popular!

You see, "great" is defined as "an extent or amount considerably above the normal or average."

What a relief!

It is *not* defined as a quality reserved for celebrities or geniuses. It is also *not* an achievement reached only by folks born into a certain lineage.

All you've got to do to be great is to be better than average. It doesn't even require you to be *massively* above the average, just "considerably."

When everything I thought was my destiny was ripped away, I decided to be great in a new way and act as a catalyst for greatness in others.

Every one of us can create opportunities to be great. You simply need to follow your own path, practice discipline, and become a silver-lining chaser!

Throw Out the "Shoulds"

I slumped in the uncomfortable chair of the guidance counselor's office, my mind wandering to where I'd rather be. Another session of tedious questionnaires awaited, in the hopes that my answers would unveil my future career. As the counselor began the scripted questions, I couldn't help but interrupt.

"Please stop," I said. "I think you're asking me all the wrong questions." She was taken back. "You're asking me about my interests but at 16 years old, I don't know enough about life to know what work I want to do for the rest of it."

Here's what I knew at that point:

I knew I wanted to be wealthy, set my own hours, travel, work in entertainment, meet amazing people, and make an impact. I wanted to do what I wanted, when I wanted, with who I wanted.

I wanted whatever career could give me *that*!

I'm grateful to finally be living the exact life I described to my guidance counselor that day, but here's the catch: To live the life you imagine, you've got to be willing to put down the "shoulds" and follow the voice of your heart.

Countless people have given me advice about how I should live.

"You should find a stable job that offers a 401(k)."

"You should stay in America; the world is dangerous."

"You should settle down and start a family."

I made a conscious choice *not* to get married so I could live the nomadic lifestyle I love.

Many people ask if I hate kids. I don't. I have twenty-six nieces and nephews and spend a lot of my time working with organizations that help children.

In 2012 I started volunteering with Dr. Cyndi Romine, founder of the organization Called To Rescue. While we were in Manila, she asked me to assist in a rescue mission.

Picture a dangerous alley controlled by pimps and drug lords. It's late at night and Cyndi and I are walking the streets looking for children who have been placed there against their will. It doesn't take long to find one. A teenage girl, dressed in nice clothes and clearly terrified, stood in a corner awaiting what could only be a horrific fate. The next day we were able to sneak in, rescue her and transport her to a safe house. Over the course of 4 years, we completed countless rescue missions, and supplied hundreds of children with clothing, living supplies and holiday gifts that they normally, humbly live without.

My work and life are like the wind, constantly changing direction and speed. I travel 100 to 150 days a year on average. If I were married with a family to think about, I would not be able to live my purpose and give a family the attention they deserve.

Here's what I know about myself:

When I feel called to do something, I experience a burning sensation inside me, and I'm fully compelled to follow it. I used to think something was wrong with me because I didn't have that burning sensation to marry or start a family.

What I know now is that we each have a role to play.

If we step outside of the roles we're meant for, to fall in line with the expectations of others, we will inevitably disappoint them and ourselves and fail to fulfill our purposes.

One of our most important tasks in life is to pay attention to those burning sensations, consider them breadcrumbs from God, the universe, or whatever resonates with you, and follow them all the way to the end.

DISCIPLINE WILL TAKE YOU PLACES MOTIVATION CAN'T

I've had the pleasure of being trained by some extraordinary people.

I noticed that the most successful people I knew shared a common habit—discipline.

They all had a structured routine from which they rarely swayed.

Greatness requires us to practice consistency rather than chasing temporary bursts of gratification.

Discipline trains us to make choices that align with our goals and require adherence to predetermined actions even when it's inconvenient.

Over time, I developed the Rated BG power hour and ultimate day routine.

Despite my location, I'm committed daily to setting aside time for work, meditation, music, reading, exercise, laughter, and music. When I am at home, I spend at least fifteen minutes every day in the music studio. If I'm traveling, I find music venues and ask if I can play a song with whatever band is on the stage.

Often, they even let me.

The point is, once you determine a routine that includes the tasks that make you feel productive, abundant, and happy, and you commit to following that routine daily, you'll find that your inspired days are adding up to a rich, fulfilling life!

IF YOU DON'T ASK, YOU WON'T KNOW

Finally, the day arrived. I stood right in front of him in awe. His Holiness, the 14th Dalai Lama personified peace, hope and humanitarianism. I was about to speak with a man that hundreds of millions of people wanted to meet.

And all I had to do was ask.

My company produces annual Humanitarian Awards, so in 2017 and 2018 I approached the Dalai Lama because we wanted to present him with our highest-ranking award recognizing his five-plus decades of humanitarian efforts.

He politely declined.

In 2019 I asked again. This time, sending a detailed deck showcasing what we'd accomplished and expressed interest in donating/volunteering with his organization as proof that we were walking our talk.

They agreed and plans were set…then COVID hit.

Finally, in 2022 I went to India and presented the Dalai Lama with the award. Being in his presence was one of the most impactful moments of my life!

How did I know I could get facetime with one of the most sought-after figures in the world?

I didn't.

But I visualized it, I manifested it, and I *asked*.

I've learned that I'd rather fail than not try. I had already fallen so many times; I knew falling again wouldn't kill me!

In my coaching work as The Dream Promoter, I see people who have settled for lives of monotony because their desires are suffocated by fear. I'm committed to helping people banish fear and rock their passion.

So many people are afraid to ask for what they want.

They're afraid of what might happen if they get it.

They're afraid of changing and of not changing and everything in between.

The year I finally went to India was not a great year. Everything that could go wrong did. All logic pointed to staying home.

But all through life, we experience what I call "Universal Taps." These are the nudges surrounding the ideas, and dreams that creep into our awareness and won't go away. Maybe you've always wanted to write a book, start a business, or meet your idol. Those passions are there to wake you up from monotony and propel you towards your purpose.

Taps are nudges whispering inspiration or warnings to help you avoid adversity. With these taps comes a choice—listen to the chatter of fear or to the inspiring voice in your heart. One of the hardest lessons for me has been discerning whether these taps were red, yellow, or green lights. It's usually later, after the silver linings have identified themselves, that I find that answer.

Fear will give you every reason to stop. Destiny will ask you to act on faith alone.

I've moved to countries without knowing the language.

I became a TV host without ever taking a class.

I started multiple successful businesses without getting a degree in business.

As author Mark Batterson wrote, "God doesn't call the qualified. He qualifies the called."

If there's a calling in your heart, follow it. If you need help to fulfill that calling, *ask!*

You may not get a "yes," but you *will* get the next breadcrumb, and it'll eventually lead you to your most fulfilling life.

GREATNESS IS IN THE SILVER LININGS

How many times have you heard yourself say, "Wouldn't it be great if…"

Imagine your life if every "wouldn't it be great if…" was

followed by decisive action, and dreams weren't just wishes but blueprints for a rich and fulfilling reality.

We named our company Be Great! because I believe every one of us deserves a life that sings with the energy of possibility and a reality that knows no bounds.

I've tried a lot of things in my life. I had some hits and even a few home runs, but it wasn't until recently that I felt like I'd won the World Series.

That's because I've learned that behind every perceived failure is a gift; an opportunity to learn and grow.

Every setback led me to a lesson: a place I was meant to be or a person I was destined to know.

True strength and success are the results of how you respond when it seems like everything is falling apart.

Do you wallow or learn? Do you turn to destructive coping mechanisms or look for the silver lining?

Do you stare behind you with regret or look forward with bright anticipation of what's to come?

The sooner we can understand the silver lining, the faster we realize that winning in life is embracing the ups *and* the downs. There are so many things we cannot control. But how we behave during victory and adversity determines the next path. Choosing to have integrity, being positive, adding value, and taking care of ourselves under any circumstances are key to making a big impact in the world.

I pride myself on filling my life with impactful experiences and was blown away to find out that this year, President Biden is honoring me with The President's Lifetime Achievement Award. But my goal is never to impress. My goal is and always will be to inspire others to pursue their greatness.

My hope is to empower others to be models, not of underwear but of service and integrity.

And above all, my mission is to create opportunities to help others *be great!*

About Bryan

Earning the nickname The Dream Promoter after helping over 250 people pursue their dreams, Bryan Gallinger is a social impact-based entrepreneur, producer, and consultant. Bryan has helped build over thirty businesses and has consulted to help develop over 100 businesses, brands, organizations, and projects. He has produced over two hundred events, including live music showcases, concerts, festivals, education, corporate, seminars, workshops, summits, conferences, pageants, personal and professional development, retreats, masterminds, wellness events, launch parties, private events, themed events, community events, awareness events, fundraisers, galas, social impact events, awards, and more.

He is a man of diverse talents and vocations having enjoyed a long career with celebrated success in various endeavors. Blending his passions as an entertainer, former athlete, humanitarian, and entrepreneur, he has built a solid network and legacy that values integrity and heart over wealth and power. Bryan is a humble man with a strong vision to inspire, empower and elevate others throughout his journey. Due to his passion for helping others, he has volunteered for over twenty-five years serving over one hundred nonprofits and social causes. Through the Be Great! network Bryan has helped raise over fifty-two million dollars for other nonprofits, social impact programs & initiatives, and charitable organizations. On March 18th, 2023, he presented the 14th Dalai Lama (Tenzin Gyatso) a Be Great! Legacy Humanitarian Award in Dharamsala, India. In May 2024 Bryan received a Presidential Lifetime Achievement Award from the White House Administration for his exemplary Humanitarian efforts almost one year before his 50th birthday.

Having led teams of twenty-plus employees and fifty-plus independent contractors, and project-managed over fifty teams, he has ample experience with business development, leadership and management. With over twenty-five years' experience in the entertainment industry, he has produced film, TV, and music internationally for over twenty-five years. Having lived in five countries and worked in over seventy-five international cities, he has had a unique understanding of different cultures. Bryan's extensive business acumen, professionalism, people skills, calm demeanor, high EQ, humanitarian passions, and strong leadership abilities earned him his second nickname Business Yoda from fellow business partners in 2015.

Currently, Bryan is the founder and executive eirector of the Be Great! Network, the founder and CEO of G.O.A.T. Consulting Group, and the (volunteer) international marketing director of Called to Rescue.

"Whatever you do in life...Be Great!"

—Bryan Gallinger

CHAPTER 6

WHEN STRENGTH ISN'T A CHOICE

Learning to Lead in the Face of Adversity

By Sunny Bert

I was packing up a cooler, excited to meet my family for a Fourth of July weekend at the lake, when the phone rang and my life changed in an instant.

Nothing prepares you for the worst phone call of your life.

I answered and heard my brother's voice. He was straining to talk, and I could tell he was crying.

"There's been an accident," he said quietly. "Mom and Dad are gone."

Life around me seemed to come to a sudden stop. My breath caught in my throat, my mind not wanting to believe that our family's world had just shattered into a million pieces.

"I was following them," he said, choking on his words. "I saw the whole thing."

In that moment, with my world forever altered by fate, a strange kind of clarity crept in. My dad, my mentor, the leader of our family and the head of the company, was gone, leaving a vast void that would need to be filled.

I was twenty-eight years old. And it would be up to me to figure out how to hold it all together.

AN EARLY LESSON IN LEADERSHIP

I was eight years old when I started working alongside my dad in his heating and air conditioning company.

I felt such pride in helping my dad, and his patience and mentorship had a huge impact on me. Each project was a testament to the strong bond between us. Together amid the hum of machinery and against a backdrop of pipes and metal, he taught me how to work, how to solve problems and eventually how to lead.

When I was about seventeen, he put me in charge. I had worked hard to earn his trust and knew the trade inside and out but tell that to the guys on the team who had decades of experience over me!

They liked me, and even looked to me for direction, but I felt very insecure and out of my element telling forty-year-old tough guys what to do.

I can remember trying to keep my voice from cracking so I could speak with some authority. I could feel their eyes on me, and even though no one was outwardly disrespectful, the bemused look on their faces told me that everyone was thinking the same thing: "Why should we listen to *him*?"

Fast-forward to today, and I've spent my whole career at the helm of teams, many of which comprised people much older than I was. Those early days prepared me for a long life of leadership roles and entrepreneurship. I bought a laundromat a few years ago and not long after, was presented an opportunity to invest in a company called Aloha Life Laundry. Aloha was helping people become entrepreneurs by teaching them how to start their own laundry service. My father had instilled in me a great respect for mentorship, so much so that I had started an apprentice program at my last company. I saw Aloha as a chance for me to continue mentoring people and helping them build lives of freedom.

Today, I am a partner in that company and director of operations. Being thrust into a position of authority at a young age taught me how to speak with confidence, how to build relationships and rally a team, how to inspire others into action and most importantly, how to embrace change with strength and courage.

Two Ears, One Mouth

Between 1861 and 1865, as the Civil War raged in the United States, Abraham Lincoln became a pillar of leadership and unity. It is said that while some Confederates saw him only as a symbol of Northern aggression, others appreciated his character.

You see, not only was Lincoln willing to listen to opposing viewpoints but he would actively seek them out to get a better understanding of the full picture. In fact, he was so committed to gaining total clarity, that when his Secretary Seward, with whom he often disagreed, fell ill, rather than using that as an opportunity to usurp him, he climbed right into the sick bed with him to ask his thoughts on the administration's next move.

You've probably heard the saying, "You have two ears and one mouth for a reason."

Leadership is often mistakenly characterized as a person standing at a podium, holding court, captivating the attention of an audience with an impassioned speech.

In reality, the greatest leaders know that sometimes the best strategy is to shut your mouth and listen!

One of the best lessons I learned as a seventeen-year-old manager is that I only knew one point of view—my own. As I listened to the men on my team share their experiences of certain situations, it hit me that every single one of us has a unique perspective, a unique set of values, and that our end goals can vary greatly.

Making the best decisions for the company meant that I had to let go of what felt like the best decision for just *me*. I had to step right into the shoes of the other people who were affected by every change, every task, every strategy.

Before, I had seen diverse insights as an obstacle to overcome. Now I see it as a gateway to a rich and dynamic dialogue that ultimately leads to solutions that benefit everyone involved.

This was a vital tool for me as a seventeen-year-old dictating to guys twice my age whose experience and credibility dwarfed my own.

It's also the secret to leading with confidence when you have no clue what you're doing and feel like a fish out of water.

You *listen*.

People are naturally fascinated by their own experiences and most human beings relish the chance to share their opinions. If you want to be able to influence anyone, resist the impulse to preach and instead, listen intently.

Not to respond, but to *learn*.

FOR TRUE LEADERS, SCHOOL IS ALWAYS IN SESSION

One day my dad asked me to go to the worksite and meet with our HVAC team to determine the next steps on a project.

"Me?" I said with a mix of pride and apprehension. "You want *me* to tell them what to do next?"

It turns out I hadn't misheard him. He was asking me to take the lead. I walked into the room with my head held high, eager to make my dad proud and prove my worth by commanding authority. But when I saw their weathered, sweaty faces, I realized that these men knew a lot more than I did about the best course of action. My speech, which I had practiced in my head on the walk over, suddenly sounded foolish and inexperienced!

I learned that day that strength isn't about always being the one with the answers. Sometimes the strongest thing you can do is admit that you don't know everything and be willing to educate yourself.

These men on our team were a treasure trove of knowledge right at my fingertips. The more questions I asked, the better positioned I was to make the same kinds of decisions my dad would make.

Their seniority was not a threat but an *asset*.

We can draw great strength from educating ourselves and steering clear of assumptions.

It was a lesson I would need to be reminded of!

After college I continued to work in the heating and air conditioning industry for many years, but decided I wanted to own my own business. I had heard that owning a laundromat was the way to go. According to a lengthy Google search and a few phone calls with different brokers, a laundromat was a great passive income stream, not a lot of work and easy to manage.

I should have realized that all the people I was talking to were business brokers who would have said just about anything to seal the deal.

The reality was that there was nothing passive about it and it was a ton of work to get off the ground.

I failed to take my own advice. I jumped into a brand-new industry without fully educating myself. If I had it to do over, I would have gone beyond Google and set up appointments with people who were *already* running successful laundromats.

I don't regret opening that business, as it led me to where I am today, but educating myself would have saved me a lot of time, money, and stress.

It was a stark reminder that knowledge is the best weapon in our arsenal for navigating *any* kind of growth or change.

LISTEN TO YOUR GUT AND JUMP IN

I was ready to rock and roll.

I had a solid business plan that outlined how I was going to purchase and operate ten laundromats over the course of a few years and my wife was happy with the projected profits of each.

As you can imagine she was totally confused when just a few months in, I told her I wanted to invest in Aloha Laundry Life and delegate a good bit of our money to growing with that company instead.

It had taken courage to build such a robust business plan. Now I needed that same courage to abandon it.

I knew I needed to persuade my wife and my financial advisor that this was all a good idea, so I gathered data, crunched numbers, and did my best to show a solid five-year projection.

Ultimately, in the absence of convincing data, I had to go with my gut. Sometimes you've got to recognize a spark of alignment when it happens and dive in.

While putting numbers on paper for my wife helped me get a clear picture of what this business venture might look like, in the end it was a passion-driven decision. It was risky.

Conventional wisdom says that you've got to take risks. If you win, you'll be happy. If you lose, you'll be wise.

I live by this motto: jump into the deep end and start paddling.

When you trust yourself enough to take a chance, not only do you build a solid sense of self-worth, but you'll accomplish more than you ever thought possible.

When it comes to facing unexpected change, there's power in trusting yourself to lead the way. You aren't always going to have all the answers laid out in front of you. That's when you've got to trust your own instincts.

If you just keep paddling, eventually you'll get to shallow end where you can stand. Paddle a little longer and you'll land on the shore. Then, when you've finally dried out, get up and jump back into the deep end again!

SEEKING CHANGE

We're often taught to accept change. In my experience, the most impactful growth happens not just when we accept change but when we seek it out.

When I was younger, I read the book *Rich Dad, Poor Dad*, and it completely shifted the way I thought about success. The most profound lesson I took from it was to make your dollars your employees. If your employees aren't functioning at a high level, you won't grow. The same is true for your money. I knew that to reach my retirement goals, I couldn't be scared to seek change, take risks, and invest in opportunities to grow.

So often, we let fear stop us from changing our lives even when change is the door that leads to everything we want.

Human beings have a tendency to fall into a trap of what-ifs.

"What if it doesn't work?"

"What if I fail?"

"What if it ends up being a waste of time or money?"

Falling victim to what-if thinking paralyzes us in a trap of indecision. When we constantly worry about what could go wrong, we rob ourselves of the opportunity to meet our full potential.

That's not to say that nothing will *ever* go wrong, only that you will survive it, figure it out, and turn it into growth.

And if you're lucky, and smart, you'll happily repeat that cycle as many times as you can as a means of creating a full and abundant life.

What I have learned over the years is that the true source of strength is *action*.

It's only in taking action that we learn what we are capable of. It's in taking action that we learn what we love, what we don't love and ultimately who we are.

You can have a well-thought-out plan and all the best intentions, but without action you're a parked car, not learning, not growing, and definitely not going anywhere.

When I was younger, *action* was a scary verb. Now I see it as a bridge to my very personal definition of success—time freedom.

I have built a life that allows me to spend time with my family, take them on trips and be at all my son's hockey games.

Whether you choose to create change or are unexpectedly thrust into it, keep paddling, because right now, as you're reading this, you have everything you need to succeed.

You have the ability to listen and to learn. You have built-in strength and powerful instincts that are always at your disposal.

And as long as you're breathing, you've got a chance to take action in the direction of your dreams.

About Sunny

From a young age, Sunny knew he wanted to be an entrepreneur. At the age of eight he began working in the family HVAC business. He chose to take the path to college rather than take over the family business, and after receiving a degree in business management he got back into the HVAC industry with a new start-up company. After an eighteen-year period of growth the business sold in 2018. Sunny stayed on board for a three-year transition period, then the entrepreneur blood in Sunny drove him to start the next chapter in his entrepreneurship. In 2021 Sunny purchased a laundromat and became a master license holder for Aloha Laundry Life. In 2022 he launched his Aloha Laundry Life business in Arizona and has seen steady growth. With the success of the business, he joined the Aloha Laundry Life team as a partner and executive in 2023 with the purpose of helping fellow entrepreneurs find success in the laundry industry. With his belief that success in business is not just about financial gain, he is able to create a positive impact and foster sustainable growth for entrepreneurs.

Sunny's passion for helping others find success has also led him to starting his business brokerage firm. His brokerage firm allows him to help entrepreneurs find a business model that they can acquire through licensing and begin to build for the future. With his experience in the business world, he offers guidance and mentorship rooted in empathy, wisdom, and practical insights. Sunny's commitment to help others achieve their goals is fueled by a deep sense of fulfillment gained by watching their transformation and growth.

In addition to professional endeavors, Sunny actively seeks out opportunities to give back to the community. Whether volunteering with local non-profits or partnering with other businesses to provide opportunities, Sunny remains diligent in his quest to make a difference in his community and the world. His unwavering dedication to help those around him succeed in the business world and beyond continues to inspire and uplift those around him.

Sunny is a dedicated husband and father to his wife, Allison, and son, Easton. He enjoys the outdoors and long road trips with his family.

To contact or follow Sunny's journey, check out his facebook (@ sunny bert) or Instagram (@alohalaundrylifegilbert), or email sunny@ cancellaundryday.com.

CHAPTER 7

THE ETHICAL EDGE

How Personal Principles Propel Achievement

By Alan Horwitz

“I must have misheard him. There's no way this is happening.”

My response was an incredulous “What?” not because I hadn't heard him clearly but because my mind could not process the words that were coming out of his mouth.

He repeated them.

“I changed my mind,” he said matter-of-factly. “I'm not going to front you the money.”

The shock hit me like a punch to the gut.

This was not a hard money lender I barely knew. I was talking to a man who was like a family member to me, a mentor and friend I'd spent the last five years working for and trusted implicitly.

For years our relationship had been close and based on an unwavering mutual respect. Now, in my moment of need, when I was on the brink of purchasing my first business and in need of the support he committed to, he turned his back on me.

My journey to this moment started when I was sixteen. My father had told me, not unlovingly, that I had to either get a job when I turned sixteen or move out! It was more of a challenge than an ultimatum, and I was ready.

My best friends were a set of twins whose mother worked at our local McDonald's so when it was time to find a job, that's where I went. I spent years at McDonald's, and when I got out of college, began to manage multiple locations, eventually moving up the ranks to personnel director and training director. After twelve years, I was ready for a change and looking for a position that allowed me to sit at the helm of an entire operation. I majored in entrepreneurship, and this was as close as I was going to get to operating a complete business.

I made contact with a franchisee who owned five high volume restaurants in California. He wanted to focus on his family and was looking for someone to take over the day-to-day operations of his company. It was a match made in heaven. For the next five years, I managed every aspect of the company, and we became very close.

Sadly, he found himself in a position of needing to sell. The new buyers were excited to take ownership of the high-volume restaurants we had grown, but not as excited to take over my salary and benefits.

I was out.

I went to McDonald's and asked if there were franchise locations available for me to purchase. There were two in Pennsylvania, but the deal required capital I didn't yet have. We would need to sell our home to fund the purchase. When I shared this with my boss, he said, "Alan, I'll happily front you the money and when you sell your house, you can pay me back."

McDonald's set a date for proof of funds, and we were good to go. Then, I received that phone call and learned that with no reason, no warning, and no empathy for my predicament, this man who was like a father figure to me, was backing out.

He would not be fronting the money after all.

It was devastating.

Not just because I was now in an agreement requiring me to show proof of funds by a specific date, but because I never could have anticipated this turn of events and the end of this significant friendship.

I was very committed to living with integrity and I thought he was too.

I learned a tough lesson that day. No matter how close you are to someone, you never fully know them. You can't always see their flaws or predict their next move. You can't always anticipate what's happening in their minds. And you for sure cannot assume that they live by the same ethics you do.

Luckily, we were able to sell the house the day before the down payment on the restaurants was due and the deal was eventually completed.

But this incident and others throughout the years have prompted me to forge a resolute conviction to live by my own code of ethics, which is really the only thing I can control.

A code of ethics is simply a set of principles that guides our behavior and decisions.

Often when life isn't going well, we can almost always trace it back to a detour from our code of ethics.

Maybe you tolerated a relationship that was clearly misaligned. Or turned a blind eye to a business deal that was just barely above the law. Maybe your gut was screaming for you to go left, and you went right instead.

I truly believe that the best way to avoid loss, regret and heartache is to form your own value system and make an unwavering commitment to live by it.

Over time I have challenged myself to create an unwritten code of ethics that I could be proud of and one I could turn to as a decision-making framework to use daily. There is little doubt in my mind that it has been the key to my success both personally and in business.

What about you?

Do you know yourself well enough to write your own code of ethics? Are you clear on your values so much so that you instantly disregard anything that isn't a match? Do you listen to your gut feelings enough to recognize when something doesn't feel right?

We can't manage what we don't measure, and we can't measure anything if we don't have a baseline to weigh it against.

Looking back, I don't think there was anything I could do to change the situation with my boss. There were no signs that he might eventually betray me. There was nothing I could have said to convince him to keep his word.

The only thing I could do was control my response, focus on my goal, and establish my baseline so that, regardless of anyone else's decisions or behaviors, I stayed true to my own values, ethics, and beliefs.

KNOW YOUR BASELINE

One of the toughest things about life is that you often learn what alignment feels like to you only when you experience its exact opposite.

The key in those moments of discomfort, shock or betrayal is to recognize the gift. Once misalignment is felt, you have the start of a new baseline to add to your code of ethics as you now know how you would prefer to feel and live instead.

When I left the restaurant business, we moved the family to Las Vegas, and I took some serious time off to enjoy my children and be with my wife. Over the years, I had cultivated a wide range of knowledge in the startup, purchase and sale of various businesses and eventually decided to become a business broker and M&A Intermediary.

I began to interview with different brokerages in Las Vegas and that's how I met the man who would become my next boss, mentor, and friend. His name is Len Krick and he's one of the most well-known and respected business brokers in the country.

He's also highly ethical and one of the most fair and honest people I know. His insights helped to shape me into the person I am today.

In the business brokerage industry, Len famously created a concept called "the Box of Reality."

The Box of Reality is essentially a set of guidelines for valuing a business. The range of what a business can sell for varies greatly but the most important thing is that the broker be able to justify the price. What Len encouraged all of us to do was to craft an extremely granular and detailed analysis, complete with verifiable supporting analytics, so that all sides of the negotiation had a crystal clear and realistic assessment of the business in question. This makes for a seamless understanding of the value of a business and allows for a very clear path forward for both a seller and potential buyer.

It stands to reason then, that we each might benefit from having our own boxes of reality as we navigate life.

If you are crystal clear on your values, your goals, your dreams, your boundaries, and all the factors, pleasant and unpleasant, of your current situation, you can move forward with clarity and confidence, fully aware of where you are, where you'd like to go and what you might need to deal with or acquire along the way.

Having your own box of reality is a means of taking realistic inventory and making decisions based on facts—not fear, not opinion, but *facts*.

Be Honest, No Matter the Cost

One of the cornerstones of my personal value system is to give honest advice.

Now that might sound like a no-brainer, but in a highly competitive industry run by metrics and transactions, honesty isn't always the top priority.

If I am committed to being of service to anyone who contacts me, I've got to give them honest advice.

It doesn't do them any good to hear sugar-coated half-truths.

I see this all the time.

A broker slaps a value on a business that they cannot possibly justify, and the client begins making all their decisions with that number in mind only to fetch less than just a percentage of it in the end.

I pride myself on being fully transparent without considering the possible fee I may be giving up.

I refuse to be misleading, to waste someone's time or to waste mine.

I can always find additional clients, but I cannot generate more time.

That's why time is our most precious and most valuable asset.

I get calls every day and being in Las Vegas, not all of them are from business I would call…appropriate. As you can imagine, I've had more than my fair share of potential clients looking to sell erotic adult entertainment related businesses or to sell businesses based on non-verifiable numbers.

In those situations, it doesn't matter how large the transaction might turn out to be, my answer is always no.

My time is limited. I prioritize time for my core pillars which are family, work, and leisure.

But boundaries aren't just for keeping shady characters or businesses out. Boundaries, when deployed tactfully and with good intention, are a form of service.

I was recently contacted by a business owner whose numbers were great. I could have made a significant commission off the sale of his business, but I encouraged him not to sell. After reviewing the data, I could see that if he stayed in business just one more year, he'd be in an even better position to sell and the difference in value could make the difference in his retirement.

Sure, it meant delaying or potentially reducing my own income, but setting that boundary was the right thing to do.

It's not all about the money to me. I'll have plenty of other clients this year.

I'd rather do the right thing.

I like to sleep at night.

PRESENCE IS POWER…AND RESPECT

The man on my right furrows his brow slightly, a possible tell of uncertainty. Across the table, another opponent repeatedly taps her fingers, perhaps a sign of impatience or nervousness. I notice another player trying to mask a smile, a tell-tale sign of a strong hand. I piece together the puzzle of body language and expressions knowing it could be the key to my victory.

Poker is a game of presence.

To win, you've got to stay fully attuned to how your opponents look, act, and speak. Every change in tone or inflection means something. It's a game I play not for the money but because it is challenging and because it keeps me mentally sharp, which is vital for success in business.

When I'm in a high-stakes negotiation, I've got to be able to read other people. I have to understand what they're saying but also intuit what they *aren't* saying!

When I'm fully present, I can adjust my strategy on the fly, addressing any concerns they have, and countering their objections if needed.

But presence is also one of the sincerest forms of respect. Whether I'm speaking to a client, my family, or my grandkids, staying present sends a message that they matter. Presence helps me build rapport and trust, showing the other party that I genuinely value the conversation and respect their time and perspective.

In the end, being attentive often leads to mutually beneficial outcomes, stronger partnerships and repeat business.

I don't play poker to win. I play to sharpen my skills and to learn. Poker offers life lessons. You can make all the correct decisions and play a hand perfectly and still lose. What is important is that you focus on playing properly and not just on winning. If you play properly in life the wins will inevitably come.

THE RACE I DON'T MIND LOSING

One of the most important principles in my personal code of ethics is balance.

I travel an average of one week every month and am lucky enough to be able to work remotely. Even when my kids were young, my wife and I traveled with and without them for four to six weeks each year. Family and balance have always been a priority.

Other brokers wear busy-ness as a badge of honor, bragging about their insane workload and trading stories of all-nighters and nightmare clients.

That's a race I don't want to be in.

What I know now is that if you're that overwhelmed, stressed out and dealing with nightmare clients, you've either failed to form your own set of principles or failed to live by them!

Living by a personal code of ethics is crucial both in business and in life. Your relationships, both personal and professional, depend on it.

But so does your self-worth and personal happiness.

It's not just about succeeding in deals or negotiations; it's about maintaining your integrity and well-being.

There is very little we can control in life. That's why it's so important that we cultivate a code to live by that is enduring and universal and that stands as a framework to turn to through every situation or decision.

I'm reminded of the words of John C. Maxwell—words I take to heart, and I hope you will too: "Policies are many, principles are few. Policies will change; principles never do."

About Alan

With over two decades' experience as a top-producing business intermediary and mergers-and-acquisitions adviser, Alan Horwitz has earned national recognition for his expertise. His career spans an impressive range of industries, from small family-owned enterprises to multimillion-dollar corporations in sectors such as casino gaming, health care, manufacturing, retail, service, and e-commerce.

Born in Indiana, Alan's passion for business ownership was ignited at an early age. His father and both of his grandfathers were business owners. Defying conventional wisdom, he became one of the first graduates with a degree in entrepreneurship from Indiana University, setting the stage for a remarkable career trajectory.

Alan's professional journey began with a twenty-five-year tenure at McDonald's, where he rose through the ranks to become a multi-unit franchisee. His entrepreneurial spirit led him to venture into business ownership in diverse fields, including advertising, consulting, and software, as well as ownership investments in various other franchised concepts.

In his second act as a business intermediary, Alan found his true calling. He approaches each transaction, regardless of size, with the same meticulous attention to detail and unwavering commitment to his clients' success. Whether facilitating the sale of a modest family business or brokering a complex corporate merger, Alan understands that every deal is of paramount importance to those involved.

Beyond his professional achievements, Alan is motivated by his love of family and by mentoring and motivating others. He finds inspiration in helping people achieve their entrepreneurial dreams, whether they're just starting out or planning their retirement. His approach to life and work is guided by a deep-seated commitment to his family and a genuine passion for his profession.

Now based in Las Vegas, Alan balances his thriving career with quality time spent with loved ones, travel, and personal interests. An avid NFL fan and poker enthusiast, he can often be found cheering on the Raiders in Allegiant Stadium or fine tuning his skills at the Wynn poker room. When working remotely, Alan divides his time between Austin,

San Diego, and Cabo San Lucas, embodying the modern entrepreneur's lifestyle.

Alan Horwitz's story is a testament to the power of perseverance, adaptability, and unwavering commitment to one's passions. His journey from a small-town dreamer to a nationally recognized business expert serves as an inspiration to aspiring entrepreneurs and seasoned professionals alike.

Contact Alan:

- Phone: 702-997-5453
- Email: ahorwitz@sunbeltlv.com or alandhorwitz@gmail.com
- LinkedIn: www.linkedin.com/in/alan-horwitz-69a08312/
- Website: www.vegasbusinessbroker.com

CHAPTER 8

THE RULE OF THIRDS

*A Powerful Formula for Strength,
Resilience, and Success*

By Nick Nanton

As the sun rose over the dusty horizon, my team and I, still buzzing with adrenaline from the previous days, readied ourselves for the long journey home.

We were in Iraq shooting a documentary about human trafficking. We had spent days interviewing people who had been abducted, trafficked, and sold as slaves to ISIS leaders. We crawled through ISIS tunnels and visited bombed-out churches and refugee camps. We were humbled and fulfilled by the work we had accomplished and were planning to take a leisurely approach to the day, relaxing before our later flight.

Until, that is, word of a different kind of adversary reached our ears.

As we walked by the front desk in the hotel lobby, we were stopped by the attendant. "Haven't you heard?" he asked solemnly. "COVID has breached our borders. There are two confirmed cases in our city now."

It was February of 2020, and COVID was just starting to sweep the globe. The last thing we wanted was to be quarantined in Iraq. We abandoned the luxury of taking it easy that morning and headed straight for the airport.

Even then, as I flew closer and closer to familiar territory, I was naive. I had heard rumblings of a worldwide lockdown and never in a million years thought it would actually happen.

It sounded like a dystopian fiction plot, not a viable possibility.

But a few weeks later, as you know, that's exactly what happened. At that time, I had a successful and growing business, more than thirty employees, a family of five to support, and a mortgage to pay. Like most Americans, I was not prepared for this and had more than one moment of total panic.

It occurred to me, though, that I couldn't solve a single problem from an anxious, fear-driven mindset. This was an unprecedented event, but it certainly wasn't the first thing to ever happen that felt totally random and out of my control.

There's a certain peace and strength in surrendering to what is, to partnering with the unexpected current instead of fighting against it.

I remembered a profound concept taught by one of my mentors, Dr. Nido Qubein of High Point University.

He teaches that *a life well-lived is lived in thirds*: one-third earning, one-third learning, and one-third serving.

It is a formula for a successful, significant, and balanced life that operates alongside the concept that you reap what you sow.

What you give emotionally, relationally, financially, and physically is refilled into buckets of support you can draw from when you need to.

It's an operating system I've used my whole life. When I've been stuck with ideas, struggling financially, or lacking inspiration, I turn to the rule of thirds for a hard reset.

The best part is it's a system for success that's free and available to you on demand. If you can align your days to include earning, learning, and serving, you will find yourself leading an abundant and fulfilling life.

A Phone Call That Blew My Mind

When the stores and schools closed and business came to a stop, I was anxious just like everyone else. Like many others, I postponed projects, cancelled events, gave money back to clients, and wondered how long we could all survive in this nose-dive economy.

It was easy to sink into glass-half-empty thinking when the news started each day with a new death toll.

Luckily, a phone call would pull me out of that breeding negativity and back into inspired action in a way I never saw coming.

I got an email from a guy named John Corcoran. He told me that our mutual friend Jack Canfield had suggested he get in touch with me. It turns out John had already been on *Oprah* and *Larry King* and was known as the teacher who couldn't read. He wanted me to make a documentary about his life and shine a light on the literacy problem in America and asked if he could call to share his story.

I wasn't sure how on earth I could top *Oprah*, but I always say yes to speaking with new people I can learn from.

That's often how I weigh opportunities: Does it meet at least two of the criteria in the rule of thirds. I knew if I spoke to John, I could learn about an issue I wasn't familiar with and possibly serve a cause.

I had no idea if it would lead to earning, but it met two of the criteria, so I was game.

During that phone call, he told me that since we started measuring literacy in America, we've never measured more than 40 percent literate. Can you imagine? We are considered by many to be the superpower of the world, but 60 percent of our citizens are illiterate or more likely what we call subliterate.

The reality is that reading is not a baked-in human skill as crawling or walking is. It doesn't come naturally. As a society, we invented words, made up characters, devised languages, and then randomly assigned sounds and symbols to it all. Our brains are not naturally wired for language. And if a kid doesn't learn to read proficiently by third grade, they often get left behind, struggling (and faking) their way through school and higher education, doing whatever it takes to avoid embarrassment.

I was fascinated. This was a systemic problem in the richest nation in the world.

I took on the film not really knowing where funds would come from.

That didn't matter. I figured if I hadn't known about these startling statistics, there was a good chance the rest of the country didn't know about them either. This film could illuminate a problem, drive resources to solve it, and hopefully change lives. I've always found that when you do something for the right reasons, and if you ask enough people to help, eventually you'll have the money.

John was so convinced that there were people I knew suffering from this issue that he said, "Nick, if you take this on, you'll get people pulling you aside at soccer games, telling you that they or someone in their lives is struggling with reading."

That's exactly what happened.

We raised enough contributions for the film to cover our crew and the production.

We held more than one hundred screenings around the world on multiple platforms.

It didn't take long for a friend to come to me and tell me that their daughter was struggling with dyslexia. They had spent a ton of money on tuition for a special school, and nothing was helping. I referred them to a reading method featured in the movie, EBLI. Within six months their daughter jumped multiple grade levels in reading.

This project was further evidence of the personal, direct, and impactful results of following the rule of thirds.

It was a reminder that no matter what life throws at us, there is great strength in broadening our horizons, taking chances, and giving back.

Do It Before You're Ready

I can't tell you how many times I've been on a stage telling my story and an audience member says something like, "That's great,

Nick, but I don't have your kind of resources. I don't know the people you know or make the money you make."

There was a time I didn't either.

The reality is you can't benefit from a formula you don't use.

I'm not suggesting you drop everything, quit your job, and follow whatever passion has captured your attention.

What I'm suggesting is that you start. Take stock in your personal and professional lives, get honest about where balance is deficient, and start adding opportunities to earn, learn, and serve.

The first documentary I made was called *Jacob's Turn*. It was just seven and a half minutes long because that was all I could afford to produce. I went on to win an Emmy Award for that short film, and it was the beginning of a deeply fulfilling and successful career in full-length documentary filmmaking.

Imagine if I had abandoned the idea for that project because I didn't have enough money to make it longer!

I was fascinated by Jacob's story and determined to tell it. My intention is always to learn and to produce content that makes a difference, and I knew I could do that even if my last name wasn't Scorsese!

It's easy for adults to get so distracted by day-to-day living that we fail to live intentionally. Instead, we are carried along by obligations and busy work, only to wake up in ten years and wonder where life went.

Have you stopped learning? Have you stopped allowing yourself to follow curiosity? Have you focused solely on earning with little thought to serving or making a difference for someone?

No judgment. We all need to repeatedly take inventory of how we are spending time. I've had a few reminders from my wife that it was time to take a break from working. After all, serving starts at home!

You see, anytime you serve another, your brain gets happy.

It rewards you with a hit of feel-good hormones. Dopamine gives you a boost of satisfaction. Oxytocin is released when an act of service bonds you to someone or creates a social connection. Then serotonin kicks in to help you sustain that state of contented bliss.

It's not surprising, then, that you feel strong and energetic as a result of this hormone cocktail, which of course inspires you to take more action and perform similar deeds.

What you're doing is creating a positive feedback loop that sets in motion a series of productive, meaningful, win-win events.

CHANGE YOUR SETTINGS

I remember it like it was yesterday. My knees would anxiously bounce up and down as the clock seemed to move at a glacial pace. My pencil tapped relentlessly on my desk as I sat there struggling to pay attention and willing the bell to ring.

I did well in school because that was expected of me, and my parents knew I was capable. But I didn't love it. My favorite subjects were lunch and recess, and my goal every day was to just get through it!

That didn't change much as I got older and trudged through law school.

I hated learning.

Or so I thought.

It turns out I just hated sitting at a desk, and that's what I thought learning was. I spent a lot of my life carrying the story that I hated learning and was a bad student.

So many of us carry labels and stories that stop us from moving forward into our full potential. That's why it's vital that we check in with our own operating systems and change the settings if necessary.

I can't tell you how many people I've met who have big dreams but say things like, "Well I would do it, but I'm not good with numbers." Or "I'd like to write a book, but I've never been good at writing."

That's just your current setting talking, and you can update it at any time!

Today, because I let go of that story, I get to learn from the best teachers in the world! I've had the chance to be educated and mentored by people including Tony Robbins, Hoda Kotb, and Magic Johnson. I've experienced more than one opportunity that most people would designate as "once in a lifetime." All I had to do was put down my limiting story and figure out how to live intentionally and in a way that aligns with my values and dreams.

Redefining our past experiences can be a real game changer.

It wasn't learning itself that I hated but the way it was packaged and dictated to me. It was a gift to discover that I was an endlessly curious soul who loves diving into new topics, just not from behind a desk.

This redefinition can be super empowering, especially when you're forced to navigate a change you didn't ask for. When life throws us into what feels like quicksand, it's tempting to fight against it. What I've found, however, is that I can change the tide if instead of saying, "This is awful," I ask myself, "How could this *not* be awful? How could I shift this to align with my values and goals?"

When COVID hit and all our events were canceled, the thought of curling up on the couch and waiting it out did cross my mind for a fleeting moment.

But then I remembered the rule of thirds and the fact that the best way out of your own misery is to focus your attention on others.

I thought about the fact that what COVID was doing was causing a bunch of problems, and as an entrepreneur, I am in the business of solving problems.

I asked myself how I could serve the folks whose businesses had been entirely disrupted by the pandemic and who were trying to figure out how to stay afloat while locked in their homes.

My team and I ended up launching a podcast division of the company that grew to seven figures fairly quickly. We were helping entrepreneurs set up their podcast shows so they could continue to do their work in a fresh way and from the safety of their homes.

I settled into a new rhythm during the pandemic by constantly looking for ways to serve, learn, and usually by default, *earn!*

> "There is a creative solution to every problem. Every possibility holds the promise of abundance."
>
> —Deepak Chopra

If there's one thing we've all learned over the last few years, it's that unprecedented change is a doorway to creative thinking.

Entire new businesses and products were launched to address the needs created by COVID.

I've heard countless stories of this happening on a personal level too.

An unexpected layoff leads to the launch of a million-dollar business idea.

A shocking diagnosis prompts someone to do their own research, which leads to a new cure.

Problems and changes are the gateway to growth.

We can handle any curveball life throws if we look for ways to serve and learn.

Just as a company works hard to create a solid company culture, when you operate by the rule of thirds, you create a healthy culture within your own life. You have a built-in barometer by which you can weigh every decision and an on-demand value system by which you can measure every opportunity.

Will this teach me something? Will this make a difference for someone else? Could this possibly lead to financial gain?

Not only have those three questions put me back on track when things got tough, but they've formed the foundation of a life and career I love.

Seeking to earn, learn, and serve reminds me that every change or challenge holds a seed of hope.

If we open our minds and focus on others, we'll find that within every unforeseen twist of fate is the opportunity to rise and thrive.

About Nick

From the slums of Port-au-Prince, Haiti, with special forces raiding a sex trafficking ring and freeing children, to the Virgin Galactic Space Port in Mojave with Sir Richard Branson, twenty-two-time Emmy Award–winning Director-Producer Nick Nanton has become known for telling stories that connect. Why? Because he focuses on the most fascinating subject in the world: *people*. As an award-winning song-writer, storyteller, and best-selling author, Nick has shared his message with millions of people through his documentaries, speeches, blogs, lectures, songs, and best-selling books. Nick's book *StorySelling* hit The Wall Street Journal Best-Seller List and is available on Audible as an audio-book. Nick has directed more than sixty documentaries and a sold-out Broadway Show (garnering forty-three Emmy nominations in multiple regions and twenty-two wins), including:

- *DICKIE V* (ESPN/Disney+)
- *Rudy Ruettiger: The Walk On* (Amazon Prime)
- *The Rebound* (Netflix)
- *Operation Toussaint* (Amazon Prime)

Nick has shared the stage with, coauthored books with, and made films featuring:

- Larry King
- Kathie Lee Gifford
- Hoda Kotb
- Dick Vitale
- Kenny Chesney
- Magic Johnson
- Coach Mike Krzyzewski
- Jack Nicklaus
- Tony Robbins
- Lisa Nichols
- Peter Diamandis
- And many more

Nick specializes in bringing the element of human connection to every viewer, no matter the subject. He is currently directing and hosting the series *In Case You Didn't Know* (season 1 executive produced by Larry King), featuring legends in the worlds of business, entrepreneurship, personal development, technology, and sports.

Nick's first love has always been music. He has been writing songs for

89

more than two decades, and his songs have been aired on radio across the United States and in Canada. He is currently ranked in the top 10 percent of songwriters in the world. His songs have been recorded by Lee Brice, Darius Rucker, RaeLynn, Joe Bryson, and many more, and have amassed more than three million streams on Spotify, Apple Music, Pandora, and SoundCloud. He received three Gold records in 2018 for his work with the global touring band A Day to Remember.

Nick has written and/or produced songs that have appeared on the following shows or in promotional commercials for:

- the Fox prime-time series *Glee, New Girl, House,* and *Hell's Kitchen*
- the MLB All-Star Game
- ABC Family's hit series *Falcon Beach*
- the CBS prime-time series *Ghost Whisperer* starring Jennifer Love Hewitt

CHAPTER 9

GIVING IT ALL TO GOD

By Nicole King

*"You'll never know that God is all you
need, until God is all you've got."*
—RICK WARREN

As soon as the song started, I broke down in tears.
The church filled with music and as I felt myself being carried away by God's presence, I prayed for guidance.

"God, tell me what to do." I whispered. The words hung in the air, and I strained to hear something. *Anything*. I would have settled for any sign that might relieve me of this confusion and fear.

How could a decision that honored my own heart be right if it meant breaking the hearts of people I loved?

I asked the question over and over and waited for God to speak to me.

I wasn't giving up. I prayed and I prayed and eventually the chaos in my mind quieted and was replaced with a small but unmistakable knowing.

Regardless of the kids, regardless of how much he would fight it, regardless of the guilt I might carry or the pain we may have to navigate, I knew.

It was time to end my marriage.

I grew up in a household that was overshadowed by depression. I wasn't depressed, so the sadness that seemed to affect everyone else felt foreign to me. It left me feeling different, lonely and hungry for the kind of love that might bring a sense of belonging.

91

It shouldn't come as a surprise then that when a friend dared me to get married during a trip to Vegas, I said yes without much deliberation as to what it all meant. I'll never forget driving home, the two of us feeling giddy and a bit dumbfounded at what we'd just done when my new husband said, "Do you have any debt?"

"No," I replied, surprised by the seriousness of the question.

"Well," he said, with what I now know was a clue of what was to come, "you do now."

One month was all it took for everything to start falling apart.

He was unhelpful, dismissive, unfaithful and sinking into substance abuse.

We both had daughters, however, so I was determined to make it work for them. I did everything I could to get him to communicate with me, but I felt like I knew the grocery clerk better than I knew my own husband.

Still, I tried to work it out. I wasn't in love with him, and my independent spirit was growing stronger every day, but the way I saw it, I had made this bed and should hold it together for the sake of our kids.

We were very poor, but I worked multiple side hustles to pay for Christmas so it looked like we had plenty. I stayed up late into the night to build my skills. I used every minute of every day as productively as possible, doing everything possible to grow as a person, take care of my children and get closer to God. I worried about every move I made and hoped my kids would somehow know that everything I did was done out of love.

As things got worse, I prayed for a miracle, but miracles are funny things. They rarely look how we think they will look.

That day in the church as I prayed for guidance, I realized that I was indeed getting my miracle.

However, the miracle wasn't a sudden infusion of love into my marriage. It was the infusion of strength I needed to finally leave it.

The Right Choice Isn't Always the Easy One

Conventional wisdom says that you'll know you're making the right choice because it will feel good to you.

I think that's quite possibly the most damaging and misleading piece of advice I've ever heard!

If you've ever had to watch your child get a shot and cried as *they* cried, you know that right decisions don't always feel good.

If you've ever had to put a loved one in a nursing home, or walk away from a dysfunctional relationship, or take a job you hated because you needed the money, you know that the right choices sometimes come with a feeling of absolute dread.

For me, the pain that everyone in my household was feeling rocked my world. Everything I was working for seemed so senseless in the face of my children's heartache. I was doing well in my career, but none of it mattered if my kids were hurting.

So how did I know I was making the right choice?

I knew because underneath the negative emotions was a sense of conviction that could only have been put there by God. This pain was part of God's plan for us, and I knew that with every fiber of my being.

Not because I felt great, but because I was being shown contrast.

One of the best ways to find out what alignment means to you is to experience its exact opposite.

I knew I never wanted to replicate the feeling I had growing up and here I was, again feeling isolated and alone. I didn't want my kids to think that this was normal and seek out relationships that mirrored mine and their father's.

At that point, no model at all was better than a broken one.

As sure as I was that this needed to happen, I wasn't so sure I was prepared for the wreckage.

My girls were terribly sad and the burden of everyone's pain weighed heavily on my heart. I had by this point built a successful career, becoming a national leader in several categories, but none of it felt exciting or worthwhile to me.

In hindsight I realized that my faith had wavered, and self-doubt had crept in, bringing with it immeasurable guilt at my decision to follow my heart.

So many women experience this imbalance.

We allow our compassion for others to betray us. We ignore the cries of our own souls so we can tend to the needs of everyone around us.

We tell ourselves it's the right thing to do, only to realize much later that what we were doing is modeling a behavior we would never want our children to emulate—self sabotage!

A year after my divorce, I went from struggling financially to being able to afford my dream apartment for me and the kids. I felt strong and capable of handling any obstacle that would come my way.

I also met my new partner, Kurt, and he encouraged me to read the Bible. I began to read scripture with my morning coffee, and we attend church every Sunday. I decided that if I couldn't figure it out on my own, I would lean into God and trust that he would make something good out of this pain.

Eventually, he did.

As I learned to free myself from the shackles of guilt and trust God's plan, new doors began to open. I quit a toxic work environment and took time to build my skills and apply for new jobs. Kurt introduced me to a company he was investing in, and I became an investor too. I didn't stop there. I went to the company's convention, volunteered my services and eventually became their CMO.

It wasn't all smooth sailing.

I made up my mind, however, to remember that every decision I made was being closely watched by my children. So, I would model faith. I would embrace change and if darkness hit, I would work tirelessly and courageously to find the light.

THE BEAUTY OF UNANSWERED PRAYERS

Women often say that we just want to be loved, but the truth is, we want to be *wanted*.

We want to be good enough, smart enough, and pretty enough.

We want to be seen and heard and respected. I realize now that my desire to be enough led me to focus too much on my career. It worked, as I was gaining the respect of my peers and climbing the ladder, but my family was falling apart.

My desire to be wanted led me to stay in a marriage that regularly insulted my self-worth.

My desire to be liked and seen as the "good guy" led me to stop speaking up for myself.

What I hope for is that my kids, and everyone for that matter, remembers that we are all loved and enough in the eyes of God.

I wasn't always a religious person, and I didn't grow up going to church. For the longest time, it made no sense to me. Who the heck was Jonah and why was he swallowed by a whale? How on earth did Abraham's wife have a baby at 90 years old!?

Little by little, however, I started to read and to learn. There isn't a single struggle I can think of that isn't depicted in the Bible and every time I hit a wall, I open that book.

At first, I had trouble praying. I felt like I was asking God for favors. I realized though that praying is a conversation and I could simply talk the same way I might share with a friend over coffee.

The answers always come; they're just not always answers we're ready to accept.

I prayed for change, for clarity, for a healed marriage, and what I got instead was preparation and training for what was to come.

As we grow, our original goals may no longer be optimal. What happens in the distance from where we are to what we want is training for what's to come.

In hindsight, every time I told God what I wanted, I eventually got it. My healing journey led me to meet Kurt, my best friend and love of my life.

That relationship led me to meet the founder and CEOs of *kathy ireland®* Licensing and MainStreetChamber Holdings, of which I became their VP of Sales and Marketing and CMO, respectively. That group introduced me to Kathy Ireland and her team, a relationship that eventually evolved into me becoming the CEO of Chamber Financial Services, dba ireland pay® Licensing.

All of this was possible because I trusted the guidance God sent me. God listens to us. If we choose to listen to Him in return, amazing things happen.

Maybe you didn't get the job because there's a better one for you.

Maybe the trip was cancelled to help you avoid disaster.

Maybe the relationship ended because your true love awaits.

We aren't meant to understand, but to listen, and to have faith that whatever guidance we hear is part of a sacred plan; one that will lead us to our destiny, if we let it.

A Master's Degree in Alignment

One thing no one tells you about hitting rock bottom is that it earns you a master's degree in alignment.

Once you've experienced the pain of isolation, abandonment and conflicting values, you become an expert in your own value system and fiercely protective of it.

I learned that my faith is my backbone. My values are my barometer. My principles are my north star.

After my divorce I was making a fantastic living in the wine and spirits industry, but it was a job that required me to be constantly entertaining, available at all hours and tolerate men who spoke to me inappropriately.

Every time I had to participate, I felt tense. I knew it was a lifestyle that no longer aligned with my values, and I needed to burn that bridge.

This happens all the time.

Our gut tells us that something isn't right.

A quickening of our pulse tells us that our boundaries are being trespassed on and our values compromised, but we stay silent to keep the peace.

We stay still to not rock the boat, and we shove down the whispers from our spirit until the whispers become a scream we can no longer ignore.

There is great strength on the other side of alignment, but we've got to be willing to pay its temporary price.

I know now that I had to go through the painful journey to find a healthier love. I had to navigate financial distress to appreciate wealth through alignment. I had to swallow my pride to rebuild my relationships.

I have to trust that any challenge I face is actually a shortcut to the life God intended for me.

ALL I HAVE

There's a song I love written by Ben Ady and Josh Howerton called "All I Have," which never fails to remind me where to turn for strength and guidance. It says the only thing I need is Jesus.

I realize now that I never needed to panic; that the entire time I thought I was experiencing a breakdown I was actually being prepared for a *breakthrough*.

If you had told me in the midst of my chaos that someday I would be working with Kathy Ireland and her amazing team, spending Sundays at church, frequently traveling with my love and our children, and doing work that is deeply meaningful to me, I probably wouldn't have believed it was possible for me.

I was too focused on praying to God to show me the next step, instead of trusting God to lead me exactly where I was meant to go.

I'm now living the exact life I dreamed of as a child. I just didn't get it on the first try and that's ok. I'm *so* proud of my growth and what's to come.

Rarely do our lives go as planned, but if we can let go of our stubborn hold on how we think life *should* be and open to how extraordinary it *could* be, we are gifted with blessings far greater than we ever dreamed of.

Faith, for me, is armor against life's storms and fuel for life's most extraordinary blessings.

It warms my heart that my own faith journey brought my father to his own. Once upon a time, my father didn't care much for people, however he went back to church at my recommendation and found a home there. Today he is known as "Salsa Mark" having gifted thousands of newcomers with homemade salsa and the teachings of Jesus!

There is no end to the joy and success we can cultivate when we open our mind, heart and spirit to God's plan.

Whatever it is you place your faith in, remember this—you cannot make a wrong decision. If something is meant for you, you cannot lose it. If you lose it, it wasn't meant for you.

So, trust your own mind, and when you can't trust that, trust your heart. When you can't trust that, trust a Higher power that sees more, knows more and wants more for you than you could possibly imagine.

No matter what life throws at you, you are always on track, always growing, and always moving one step closer to the life you were meant to live!

About Nicole

Nicole King brings a wealth of experience to the intersection of business leadership and spiritual alignment. With a background in sales, marketing, and strategic business consulting, Nicole has consistently set new standards for innovation, creative problem-solving, and out-of-the-box thinking. Her journey has been marked by a commitment to client education, empowering others with knowledge to make well-informed decisions.

As the chief marketing officer (CMO) at MainStreetChamber Holdings, Nicole emphasizes growth as an essential element. She believes that without growth, we stagnate. Advertising, in her view, is the heartbeat of visibility, and she consistently goes beyond expectations to provide strategic insights and personalized attention to clients partnering with MSCH.

Nicole's chapter in the book "Strength," drives the importance of alignment with faith in the business world. Drawing from her extensive experience, she explores how spirituality can infuse purpose, resilience, and authenticity into entrepreneurial endeavors. Nicole emphasizes the alignment of our stories with a higher purpose.

When she's not shaping business strategies, Nicole enjoys frequently traveling and spending time with her family. Whether it's developing new processes or helping companies overcome challenges, Nicole's passion lies in empowering people to succeed while becoming the best versions of themselves.

Keep up with Nicole:
Instagram: @marketinghelp247
Website: www.marketinghelp247.com

CHAPTER 10

THE PURSUIT OF HAPPINESS

By Christopher M. Dugan Jr.

"**Y**ou're going to celebrate your eighteenth birthday in an orange jumpsuit, eating your cake in your jail cell!"

My family's harsh words ran through my mind on repeat, mocking me, as rain poured through the football bleachers, soaking my bed of concrete.

"Well," I thought half sarcastically and half in resignation to my dire circumstances, "at least my clothes are getting washed."

I was thirteen years old, and it had been fourteen months since I left my mother's home, determined to escape the abusive hand of my stepfather and the crushing disappointment I felt in my mother's unwillingness to stand up for me.

My mom and dad split up when I was six. My dad moved to Florida, but to us, he may as well have moved to the moon. We rarely saw him, and my mom coped with the divorce by distracting herself with relationship after relationship and avoiding paying too much attention to me, my brother, and my sister.

Perhaps we were painful reminders of a life gone wrong.

One day, when the current man in her life raised his hand to my sister, I stepped in. A fight broke out, and much to my shock, my mom did not take my side.

I left the next day.

I slept in bus stops and under bleachers and occasionally jumped from couch to couch.

It was a rock-bottom story waiting to happen—poor kid with a dysfunctional family, living on the streets.

So you see, statistically, I shouldn't even be here.

Data would tell you that a kid with my background should be incarcerated, addicted, or dead.

But I wasn't going down like that.

I was going to prove my family wrong. Not only would I avoid celebrating my eighteenth birthday in jail, but I would succeed beyond anyone's wildest expectations. I would be the one to break this generational pattern of lack and bitterness.

And I'd do it before my twenty-fifth birthday.

A WAKE-UP CALL

I was fourteen years old when I met my wife.

Sounds crazy, I know, but the second I saw her, I knew she was the one. She was way out of my league and told me so as she tossed her silky black hair over her shoulder, laughed her infectious laugh, and walked away. She was amused. I was devastated.

They say when you know, you know. And I knew.

I pursued her relentlessly, wrote her notes, sent her flowers regularly (she sent them back), and told her over and over that we were meant to be together. Eventually, either out of pity or exhaustion, she agreed to go out with me. We were sixteen at the time. I think perhaps this was my first lesson in entrepreneurship. Never give up on a goal!

The challenge was that she is Mexican and I'm white. Her parents vehemently disapproved of our relationship. At this point, however, we were in love, so we moved in together when we were seventeen.

I was working at a car wash at the time and worked hard enough that I received multiple promotions. It's a good thing too, because a year later, at just eighteen years old, I found out I was going to be a father.

I was working full time and going to school and took a second job at Honda. I was determined to support my family and was smashing sales records, with nearly half a million in sales in my first year as a service adviser. In between client meetings I was doing calculus homework.

One week before the baby was due, I was able to rent us a tiny two-bedroom house. I had just turned nineteen and was making enough to pay our bills, rent a home and own two cars.

I was overjoyed to be a dad but was painfully aware of the responsibility I now had to keep this little roof over our heads. I worked seven days a week, leaving the house at 6 a.m., getting home at nine or ten at night, and rinsing and repeating the same process the next day.

I couldn't even attend my college graduation because I had to work, but I was proud of what I had accomplished.

Then COVID hit.

I was immediately laid off, and as the harsh realization that I was totally replaceable set in, I coped by losing myself in video games for weeks on end until some tough love from my wife brought me back to reality.

I eventually landed a job as a store manager for Monro Auto, making $80,000 a year at just twenty years old. The catch was that I was working eighty hours a week. Finally, we weren't just scraping by. We could go to dinner, buy new clothes, and fill our refrigerator. In August of that year, I took my wife and son on our first vacation. I had never left the tristate area, had never been on a plane, and had never seen the ocean.

It was on that vacation that I realized that my son, who was already two years old, barely knew who I was. As we sat by the ocean, drinking in the scent of salt water mixed with the warm air, I watched my little boy play in the sand, and my heart broke.

This could not be what success felt like. I no longer wanted to just focus on making money.

I wanted to know my son.

The Obstacle Became the Way

The next few weeks were the portal to an entire life transformation. I was determined to work from home and went through a string of failed attempts and remote job applications that went largely ignored. My wife went back to work, leaving me in charge of the baby…and the laundry.

We had moved to a very remote part of the state. There were no stores, no supermarkets, and the nearest laundromat was an hour away.

It drove me crazy. Doing laundry was a huge ordeal that required me to pack up the baby, drive an hour, wait for it to be done, and drive an hour back. I dreaded laundry day. Total waste of time! Again and again, I found myself wishing there were a service that allowed me to ship my laundry to the laundromat and have it done and shipped back to me.

And that wish was the start of a million-dollar idea.

That's how most life-changing ideas start—as a problem and a wish for a solution.

I realized that thousands of people lived in rural areas, didn't have laundry hook-ups in their homes, and probably had the same challenge and frustration that I did.

I found out that 19 percent of houses are not equipped for laundry. I couldn't believe it!

I got busy. I called FedEx and UPS, pitched my model, and built solid relationships. I called more than ten thousand laundromats myself, and before long, Laundry Scoop had scaled to all fifty states!

It was a huge success, but the most important thing to remember is that it wasn't born from trying to make a quick buck. It was born from a desire to solve a problem.

In July 2023 I was contacted by the CEO of Aloha Laundry Life, an amazing company that helped people become laundry service entrepreneurs. All our interests aligned. We merged and became one. Aloha acquired Laundry Scoop and I became CTO of the company.

The internet is flooded with "get rich quick" strategies but chasing after money is a recipe for disaster and burnout. The true secret to success in business, and in life for that matter, is to be driven by a sense of purpose and passion and the desire to solve problems for other people.

The true secret to thriving? Set out to make a difference, not a quick buck.

DON'T BELIEVE THIS HYPE

One thing I've noticed when I talk to people who have dreams of changing their lives and starting a business they love is that they tend to come up with every reason it would never work.

They say they don't have the time.

They say they don't have contacts.

But an overwhelming number of them say they don't have the money.

There's a misguided belief that launching a business requires substantial capital, a theory probably perpetuated by the equally misguided phrase "You need money to make money."

It's just not true. I started Scoop with just $4,000 in the bank, and it is now a national enterprise. I've started drop-shipping businesses with as little as $50.

Sure, having a little more investment capital helps, but what really propels you forward is a mix of grit, determination, and a hunger so deep it inspires you to work hard and to do what it takes—*whatever* it takes—*until* it takes.

And it's true for any goal you have. Maybe you want to heal from a broken heart, find a partner, lose weight, or write a book. What you need more than anything else is an unwavering focus on that goal.

Abraham Hicks wrote, "It's as easy to create a castle as it is a button. It's a matter of whether you're focused on a castle or a button."

Figure out what you want. Want it enough to focus on it as though having it is the only option. Want it so badly that you are willing to devote yourself entirely to its inevitable fruition.

That's what it takes. Not money.

But heart. Grit. And a stubborn refusal to settle for anything less than what you dream of.

Success Is Not a One-Man Show

If you ever decided to write a book, you would likely be encouraged to join a writers' group.

Start a diet, and you'll be encouraged to diet with a partner so you can hold one another accountable.

Begin a twelve-step program, and you'll attend meetings with other people who share a goal of sobriety.

There's a reason that we are encouraged to involve other people in our goals and dreams.

None of this is meant to be a solo act.

When I first started Laundry Scoop, I was totally alone. I was a national organization and was the *only* operator. I called more than ten thousand laundromats myself to enroll them in the program. I handled all my own marketing and operations. It was exhausting and unsustainable.

When Aloha acquired the company, I suddenly had a team to work with and delegate to and that freed up a lot of head space for new and innovative ideas to take root.

If you run a business, hire as fast as you can, before you think you're ready and even if you think you can't afford it. Your employees will make you money.

If you are not running a business but have a personal goal, tell someone. Immediately. Forming a support system is probably the most underrated success strategy I can think of.

And not forming one is a cop-out exit strategy.

When no one knows that you want to lose weight, or quit your job, or whatever, you can easily give up without the shame of accountability.

When you declare your intentions and involve other people, you are much more likely to stay the course and eventually hit or surpass your target.

There is extraordinary strength in numbers.

SUCCESS IS ON THE OTHER SIDE OF PATIENCE

I remember it like it was yesterday.

My grandfather and I sat in silence, our breaths blowing clouds in the cold air. The metal handle of the rifle chilling my hands and the anticipation building with each passing moment.

We were hunting in the woods, and hours had passed without a single sighting of the buck.

Leaves would rustle, and I'd snap to attention, only to see a bird hopping around a few yards away.

My grandfather sat there, silent and motionless, certain that our patience would eventually pay off.

And it always did.

Hunting and fishing with my grandpa are some of my fondest memories, but what I realize now as an adult is how much of that time was spent waiting. Sitting. Watching. And how important it was to not get discouraged and give up.

Everyone around us would pack it up for the day, but we'd wait. And we'd always get our shot in the end!

Success is often on the other side of a resolute commitment to exercising patience.

I could have given up a million times. When there was no money and a baby on the way, I wanted to disappear! But I didn't.

I stayed patiently focused on my desire to build a better life.

I learned very early on, sitting in the woods or on the dock with my grandpa, waiting for a fish to bite, that success comes when you make decisions based not on how you feel but on what you ultimately want.

CHANGE—AND BREAK—THE NARRATIVE

My parents did the best they could with what they had, but I always knew I wanted to be different.

Growing up, I was surrounded by adults who didn't really set big goals for themselves, who settled for a lot less than they wanted and then spent their lives complaining about it.

I knew I didn't want to live that way.

Once I moved out of the house, I never once asked for a handout.

The odds were against me, but you never have to accept the odds.

You can decide at any moment to break every pattern that's holding you back.

When I was working full time, going to college, and taking care of a baby, I was so tempted to quit school. But I didn't want to be the excuse my son would throw at me someday when *he* wanted to quit.

Every decision I make is based on lessons I want my kids to learn.

Every goal I set is meant to help me stretch to a new level of growth.

My journey has been littered with every imaginable obstacle, but I never gave up my vision of a reality filled with love, success, purpose, and a happy, healthy family.

So no, I will not be spending any birthdays in an orange jumpsuit in my jail cell. I'll be spending them at my home, with my wife and our beautiful children, enjoying the life of abundance we've created.

In the end it's not about where you came from, how many times you've fallen, or how high the odds are stacked against you. What matters is that you get up and decide to keep going.

All our lives, boulders will be thrown into our paths. We can stop. Or we can climb them.

I will never let those boulders stop me. I will always climb them. And when they stack extra high, I will keep climbing until I reach the top.

And I hope you will too.

The view is fantastic.

About Christopher

Christopher M. Dugan Jr.'s dedication to his family has driven him to build a series of successful ventures. In 2020, after his first-ever vacation, Christopher found himself reevaluating what defined his success. He made the pivotal decision to leave a high-paying automotive management position due to its demanding schedule, pursuing a remote opportunity to spend more time with his wife and son.

At only fourteen years old, he was accepted into an education program called P-TECH, partnered with the Chamber of Commerce. During this time, he worked with top brands like Gillette Creamery, MediaCom, and Autodesk, learning about their challenges and pitching his solutions within their boardrooms.

Chris is the founder of several online companies that he and his team operate from their homes, including, but not limited to, Laundry Scoop, AHF Depot, Dugan Homes, and Online Venture Hunt.

At twenty-three years old, Chris sold his first company, Laundry Scoop, an online mail-order laundry service, to Aloha Laundry Life, a larger laundry pickup and delivery chain. Following this acquisition, Aloha Laundry Life hired Chris as their Chief Technology Officer, and he has since become a majority shareholder and co-owner of the company.

Today, Chris is on a mission to fan the flames of entrepreneurship across America, envisioning a future where every individual, regardless of their circumstances, has the chance to become a thriving business owner. Through his social media presence, motivational speaking, authoring books, and creating business opportunities through his companies, Chris aims to empower and inspire the next generation of entrepreneurs.

You can contact Chris across all social media platforms using the handle @successist_duga:

LinkedIn: www.linkedin.com/in/christopher-m-dugan-jr/

Website: www.successist-duga.com

CHAPTER 11

SLAYING THE GIANTS

By Peter J. D'Arruda

I picked up the phone on the first ring, recognizing the number of one of the financial advisers I'd been working with.

My team and I were contracted through a field marketing organization (FMO) to build radio shows for fifty-two advisers, and this guy was one of my favorite clients.

"Coach Pete," he said, in a tone that immediately put me on edge. "I've got to tell you something."

What he said next came as a complete shock to me. I sat there, stunned into silence as the reality of the betrayal set in.

Since my involvement with this company, over nearly 8 years, most of their advisors were generating five to six times more revenue than before their shows. It was a huge success. So successful, it turns out, that the company wanted me gone.

With me out of the picture, they could steal my model and retain all of the profit for themselves.

I received several calls over the next couple of days from loyal colleagues informing me that the company was soliciting business and employees away from me.

They stole everything.

My entire staff left and that year I lost one million dollars in revenue.

One million dollars.

I was dumbfounded, but mad as hell.

This company had hired me to produce these radio shows to

help their clients market their services. I did exactly what I was hired to do, and it was hugely successful.

And they were repaying me by lying, stealing, and throwing me out of the picture.

If something like that has ever happened to you, then you know the drill.

At first, you're shocked. Then a kind of incredulous sadness and self-doubt kicks in. You wonder, "Were there signs? Should I have seen this coming?" And then once you've convinced yourself that there were no signs and this was just a massive betrayal, that's when anger comes calling.

Now there are two types of anger. The type that makes you stagnant and bitter, and the type that lights a fire!

I made up my mind to rebuild bigger than ever. I started my own media company, Broadcasting Experts LLC, and it took off like a rocket ship.

Today, I still run that media company, and I'm also the manager and founding principal of Capital Financial Advisory Group LLC in Apex, North Carolina.

For years I've had my own radio show called Financial Safari, which is real-life financial guidance on the things most people screw up with a bit of comedy thrown in to keep this heavy topic light. I'm proud to say it's a hit, and I know this business inside and out.

The betrayal I experienced turned out to be a huge blessing. It was the catalyst for the next level of growth. The stubborn resolve to make a comeback opened the door wide to fresh and innovative ideas that helped my company scale and *fast*.

They took my staff, and they took my money, but they couldn't touch my drive.

I was David against Goliath. And I was winning.

SLAYING THE GIANT

In case you're not familiar with the story, David and Goliath is the tale of a young shepherd, David, who is chosen to fight the fierce giant Goliath. The victor would determine the outcome of the battle between the Philistines and Israelites. David was small in stature and armed with just a slingshot and a few stones.

This was a seemingly impossible feat, and everyone assumed he was a goner.

In a remarkable display of valor and courage no one saw coming, David slayed the giant with a single shot to his forehead.

I've been slaying giants my whole life.

I was born in Delaware, but my family moved around a lot, and we didn't have much money. A lot of our meals consisted of peanut butter and government cheese. My father was a nuclear physicist, and we went wherever the teaching jobs were. I was always the new kid and as if that's not hard enough on its own, I was poor and had a speech impediment that made me sound like Elmer Fudd. I got beat up and bullied but I overcame it when I discovered two of my superpowers—listening and a sense of humor!

Once I found an audience, I didn't let them go and often got in trouble for talking too much. It makes total sense that I talk now for a living.

But when I first started marketing myself as a speaker and radio host, no one wanted me. At the time I was a no-name guy fighting against the big wigs for airtime. Eventually, someone took a chance on me, and the rest is history.

As a financial planner, I've faced Goliaths my entire career. I was a small business owner competing against household names like Edward Jones and Morgan Stanley.

Fear would have finished me in the first year if I hadn't mustered up the courage to forge ahead, holding the vision in my mind of the kind of life I wanted to live.

Maybe you've encountered a few giants of your own. They take various forms. A divorce. A job termination. A scary diagnosis.

In those moments we feel so small, scared, and ill-equipped to face any of it.

And that's exactly why we must press on. Greatness can come from the most unlikely moments.

Ultimately, the story of David and Goliath serves as a reminder that nothing is impossible, and no obstacle is insurmountable when we meet it with determination and faith.

But how? From where do we pull this courage and faith?

It turns out that many of the principles I teach on building wealth are applicable to building anything you want in life.

A Combat Lesson to Live By

Under a dark, moonless sky, WW1 soldiers moved slowly and steadily towards enemy territory. Fifty feet at a time they pressed on, stopping to dig their spades into the soil and carve out trenches that would act as shields against enemy fire.

When the atmosphere again grew quiet, they'd advance fifty feet more and dig again. It's a military tactic known as "advance and protect."

The idea is to always be moving forward but not recklessly.

It's advice I often give my clients. Pensions are a thing of the past. This generation can't rely on the same kind of safety net that kept our parents and grandparents secure.

But we can't let that fact stop us from moving forward.

I always advise my clients to move forward with investing and taking educated risks while at the same time protecting what they accumulate along the way. They can do this by, for instance, placing it somewhere not readily accessible, but growing for a guaranteed lifetime income stream in a special annuity I call a "Financial Fill-Up Strategy.

What you can't do is stop and on the flipside, you can't be reckless.

You've got to invest, diversify, and protect all at the same time.

Maybe you've got your money protected and that's great, but in what other ways might you be vulnerable?

Maybe you're building a business, and you need to watch your budget, so you stay still, not investing in marketing or staff. You won't grow with that mindset.

Maybe it's your boundaries that need some work. Maybe you have a pattern of recklessly letting anyone and everyone get too close. Protect your boundaries.

Whatever your goal is, always be moving forward, but stay aware of your potential vulnerabilities and keep yourself safe.

This is where self-awareness and self-control come into play. Most successful people who have things they don't want to lose lock them up in a safe and forget about them while they move onto new goals and acquisitions.

What matters to you? Whether we're talking about $100,000, your business, your self-worth or your boundaries...

Advance and protect.

THERE IS STRENGTH IN KNOWING YOUR WEAKNESS

Back in 1979 we spent the entire summer up in New England with my grandparents, the highlight of those trips for me was getting to spend time with my uncle George.

I looked up to him. He was cool and funny and would entertain us all and then head back to his home in Boston. One weekend though, he didn't leave. I found out that there was no more home in Boston.

My uncle had lost all his money in the stock market. Every penny. He was living with my grandparents now.

To see my strong uncle humbled in that way was a shock and I made up my mind that I would never be in that position. I would educate myself and do everything I could to plan a secure future.

My uncle never recovered and passed away in the same house he was born in.

My main goal as a financial planner and educator is to ensure that my clients don't run out of money while they're still alive.

I see way too people many trying to figure it all out on their own. They read articles here and there, follow advice they hear on the golf course and make *big* decisions without considering or understanding long-term ramifications.

It's only after they realize that they've spent too much and started too late that they pick up the phone to call me.

At that point, I look at everything, clean up the mess and make sure they never have to worry about having more years left than money.

No matter what you're trying to do—start a business, reach a fitness goal, repair a relationship—don't forget that there are people out there trained to help with the exact goal you're trying to reach.

Ask for help.

When my tooth hurts, I don't pick up a drill, I call a dentist!

It's tempting to go it alone, but there are always people out there who have seen what you're going through, overcame it already themselves or are trained and certified to solve the exact problem you have.

"Trust but verify" is a principle in financial planning that emphasizes the importance of both trusting financial professionals while also verifying their advice and actions. While you've got to trust the person handling your money, it's equally important that you take an active role in understanding your situation and moving forward.

The same is true for any mission you're trying to accomplish.

By adopting a "trust but verify" approach with any goal, you can strike a balance between leaving it to professionals while staying self-aware and responsible. This approach promotes transparency, accountability, and informed decision-making.

It's incredibly empowering to ask for help while simultaneously educating yourself.

Expertise is a weapon against every giant that comes your way.

But you've got to call on it before it can come to your rescue.

KNOW YOUR RED ZONE

In financial planning the "red zone" typically refers to the critically important period leading up to and immediately following retirement, usually falling at age fifty-five and above.

This is a time when people are extremely vulnerable as they are likely earning less income but facing increased costs in healthcare and other things and due to their age, they'll have less time to recover before needing to dig into their savings.

This is one of the reasons we encourage people to work with an RICP® (Retirement Income Certified Professional) as early as possible so that when they reach the red zone, they are prepared rather than panicked. (If you would like your very own Lifetime Plan, feel free to visit my website today and request a *free* consult with me and my team. We are available nationally. Just visit www. CoachPete.com.)

What I've found over the years is that life is riddled with red zones.

Every relationship goes through phases where communication dips and tempers flare and usually, there are early indicators that a rough patch is coming. But life is busy, and egos are strong and too often we ignore those red zone clues until it's gotten so bad, a once happy couple reaches the point of no return.

It happens with our bodies too. We recognize symptoms of burnout but keep going. We ignore that pain in our side because we're too busy to go to the doctor. Soon, what was a totally minor and curable issue is requiring surgery and totally disrupting our lives.

Sometimes it's our money. A card is declined because there is no more credit. A late fee goes ignored and compounds. These are the whispers meant to protect you, but you've got to listen to them.

Think of all the times in your life you've said to yourself, "Something doesn't seem right," and then pushed that thought down and went on with your life. Then, a few months later, something happens, and you realize you were right. You should have listened to that little voice trying to steer you in the right direction!

One of the keys to both happiness and success is becoming so radically self-aware that you immediately know when something is "off." But you can't stop there. You can't sit on it, ignoring all the signs, moving forward when all the clues are screaming at you to stop and take stock. When something feels off, you are being warned that a red zone is imminent.

Stop what you're doing and take immediate action!

Life is kind in that it gives us clear warnings. Don't be the person that ignores the danger sign and ends up driving off a cliff!

THE KEY TO BEING UNSINKABLE

When I'm working with clients, I often encourage them to deploy a "core and explore" philosophy.

What this means is that they should be sure to have a core amount of money they don't touch. This is their money that will support them in retirement. The rest of the money is used to explore riskier investments.

I try to live by this personally too.

I know my core character, and no one can take that away from me. I take risks and chances and try new things that challenge me, but my core character and value system remain unchanged and untouchable.

I will always be kind. I will always fight for the underdog and do everything I can to protect my clients and family. I will always be abundant because I made up my mind years ago that I'm just not available for poverty.

Once you know your core character, you can live life boldly knowing that no matter what happens, or how much changes, it cannot affect you in your core unless you let it.

They say that everything happens for a reason, and I don't always like the reason.

But the secret is to go to sleep and wake up in a brand-new day, committed to keeping your core intact, determined to keep your red zones in check, and with a fierce determination to slay any giant that comes your way.

About Peter

Peter J. D'Arruda, MRFC®, RICP®, is a Registered Financial Consultant and Investment Advisor Representative, and is manager and founding principal of Capital Financial Advisory Group LLC in Apex, North Carolina.

Popular public speaker, nationally syndicated radio show host and accomplished author, Coach Pete has appeared on numerous national television programs and has been featured in major national publications to discuss his personal philosophy on wealth management and applying various financial solutions. He has won four Emmys and seven Tellys.

A fiduciary with over thirty-two years' experience in the financial services industry, he is former two-time president of the International Association of Registered Financial Consultants (IARFC).

Known as Coach Pete to most of his clients and radio show listeners, his lifetime goal is to assist his clients in achieving the levels of success they desire. He founded Capital Financial to help his clients "cross the street of life." He and his team strive to help their clients take the worry out of living in retirement by taking a systematic approach to lifetime income planning.

Coach Pete's radio show, *Financial Safari*, can be heard weekly on stations nationwide. He has been a guest on CNBC, FOX Business, Bloomberg, and CBS Radio. He has been interviewed for advice on columns in *The Wall Street Journal*, *USA Today*, Smart Money, TheStreet.com, and others.

Coach Pete has written eight books and cowritten six more. Four of his books have reached the best-seller list on Amazon.

Pete is a graduate of The University of North Carolina.

Contact Coach Pete today for your very own TOTAL RETIREMENT PLAN™ at CoachPete.com.

About Pete

CHAPTER 12

IF THERE WERE A WORLD FULL OF YOUS, WOULD YOU WANT TO LIVE THERE?

By Patricia Lynn Watson

It was supposed to be a routine doctor visit. I'd be examined, they'd tell me everything was fine, and I'd forget all about it for a year until the next annual appointment.

Only that's not what happened.

A few days later, my phone rang.

"Patricia, I need to tell you two things."

My doctor's voice sounded tense, her tone suggesting that for whatever she was about to tell me, I might want to sit down.

"We've found cells that could be cancerous."

My heart stopped for a minute, but always the optimist, I exhaled, holding onto the notion that only further testing could confirm any kind of dire diagnosis.

"Ok," I said hesitantly, "and the second thing?"

"You're pregnant."

The first shock I had managed with an odd sense of calm. This second bit of news knocked me off my feet. I already had a two-year-old, so what now? I was a single parent struggling my way through school as it was.

I can tell you that neither cancer nor pregnancy were in my plan at that time, but that's how life works, right? God's timeline, not ours.

Not long after that phone call, I went through a series of tests that confirmed Ovarian cancer. By that time, I was four and a half months pregnant. I spent days researching the effects of radiation treatment on fetuses and what I found brought no comfort.

I knew in my heart that this child was destined for greatness, and it was my job to usher that in. It was the same feeling that I had with my oldest. I just *knew* this was part of a GREATER plan.

There was no way I was putting this baby through brutal cancer treatments whose long-term side effects were still largely unknown.

I told no one. If my family knew that the choice was my life or the baby's, they'd want me to choose myself.

It was a heavy secret to carry. When I was six months pregnant, I wrote letters for my unborn child and to my two-year-old Mikyle to open on their twenty-first birthdays. I wanted them to know how much I loved them from day one. I wrote letters of gratitude to my family.

I did a lot of painful things just in case my decision to protect my child led to my death.

But most of all, I prayed.

"God if this is your will, I won't question it. I don't understand it, but I'm trusting you to see me through."

And he did.

That was nineteen years ago. Today I am a lobbyist and own an advocacy firm called Tew Advocate. We recently won fifteen million dollars in funding for family and children's services. I also own a graphic and print company called Hood Adjacent Tees.

My oldest son Mikyle will graduate in 2025 from RIT with a dual engineering degree. He was valedictorian of his class.

My youngest son Spencer, bright and hilarious and standing at over seven feet tall, is going into his second year at UMES and following in my footsteps of being a Psychologist upon graduation 2027.

Since that first cancer diagnosis, I've been diagnosed every two to three years; six times in total.

Some say it's a miracle I'm still here. But I attribute my luck in part to the life lessons God continually gifts to me.

Lessons that wake me up when I'm asleep, remind me of my blessings when I'm feeling victimized and ultimately, walk me home to my heart.

BE THE CHANGE

I remember it like it was yesterday.

He was standing on a street corner in dirty clothes and broken shoes. His face looked gaunt and hungry. It was clear to me even at the age of four that this was a man whose life had gone off course.

My mother, whose generosity knew no bounds, kept a pile of blessing bags in our car; small bags filled with toiletries and a few dollars. She rolled down the window and handed him one. His face broke into a smile as though it had been years since he received kindness from anyone.

Giving is part of my DNA. I believe that when you are blessed, it's mandatory to bless others.

I love the Random Acts of Kindness movement, but I'm also a big fan of FAST acts of kindness. You don't have to spend hours volunteering at a non-profit. You don't have to spend money paying for the drive-through order for the car behind you.

Just a two-second, genuine compliment can bless someone else with the strength they need to get through the day.

There are so many ways to give.

When I got married ten years ago, my husband and I were already both established and we didn't need dishes and towels!

We asked instead that our guests meet us at a shelter and bring items for the women and children. I was thrilled to find out that a few of my friends adopted this idea for their weddings and birthdays!

One of the best things you can do when you're feeling down or weak is bless another.

Your choice to do something kind might be the only source of strength someone else can grab onto.

And one of the best times to be charitable is around people who aren't!

One of my favorite quotes from Rumi says, "Wherever you stand, be the soul of that place."

No matter what's happening around you, or how rude or grouchy someone is, you can choose to be a source of love and light.

You can always be the change you want to see.

It's **OK** to Not Be **OK**

Most of us are guilty of it.

We scroll through the Facebook newsfeed and then fall into painful bouts of "comparisonitis."

Sometimes you're having an ok day until Facebook shows you how your life "should" be.

You see Lisa from high school taking a luxury vacation and wonder why you never get to take one.

Your mood nose-dives as you see people posting pictures of their glamorous career, their perfect body, and the gourmet meal they just cooked.

Because there you are, navigating a divorce, fighting an illness, or nursing a broken heart and this wasn't how life was supposed to go!

Social media does a fantastic job of tricking us into thinking that the only kind of life worth living is one that's carefully curated, Pinterest perfect and Instagram-able.

Says who?

Life, by nature, is dark and then light. It's brutal and then beautiful.

It's ok to not be ok.

The ebbs and flows are what make us profoundly human and the only guarantee we'll ever get from life is that it will always, inevitably, change.

Go ahead and celebrate Lisa's vacation pictures because next month she may be posting and asking for prayers!

Share your moments of darkness because your willingness to be real might give someone else permission to forgive themselves.

There's no rulebook for living a great life.

There are no rule books for love, parenting, work or for what a successful life looks like

That's great news, isn't it?

When there's no rule book, you get to write your own.

Write Your Own Rulebook

"The authentic self is soul made visible."

—Sarah Ban Breathnach

Writing your own rules for life allows you to live authentically.

When you create your own rules, you release expectations or other people's opinions, which leaves you free to do what genuinely makes you happy.

You don't need to be a scholar to write your own rule book. The formula is super simple.

Figure out what makes you happy and do more of it!

If something makes me happy, I immediately write it down. If I catch a glimpse of myself in the mirror looking cute, I'll make a note to wear more pink.

If I notice that sleeping in an extra 30 minutes made me feel more productive and energetic, sleeping in is now a rule.

Your rulebook should be a mix of values and preferences.

Most of us are good at living by our values.

We know that part of our personal rulebook includes being kind, having integrity, and keeping our word.

We tend to slack off, however, when it comes to our dreams and preferences, demoting them to selfish whims.

One of the best ways to feel strong is to cater to your wants, no matter how small and insignificant they seem.

If something makes you happy, it raises your energetic

frequency which projects positivity to the people around you, which ultimately means you've made an impact just by honoring your desires!

I'm committed to living a life that is rooted in service and inspiring others.

Visiting the oncologist has, unfortunately, become a routine part of my life. I feel like a bit of a veteran in the waiting room. I see the patients there carrying a sudden and unwelcome awareness of their own mortality and my heart aches for them.

I cannot take away their cancer, but I can give them a purpose that goes beyond survival.

And it's advice that perhaps you'll use to write your own rulebook for life.

I tell them to live their life in such a way that if they died, they'd be OK with what's written in the obituary.

Conduct yourself in such a way that everyone's last memory of you would be that you were an inspiration.

How are you spending your time? What are you bringing to the world, either on a small scale at home or a large scale in your community? What dreams have you let go?

If you were to read your own obituary today and the words within it leaving you feeling full of regret, it's time for a change!

Let that be your strength and motivation to live differently, dare courageously, and love with your whole heart.

And to do it by your *own* rules.

YOUR WORST IS SOMEONE ELSE'S WISH

Winter in Baltimore is marked by piercing winds and frigid temperatures that blanket the streets in ice.

I'd just gotten out of my car at work when I saw a patient struggling to walk. I rushed to help, but when I reached her, her feet slipped on the ice. She fell right on top of me, and I came down hard on the snow-covered pavement, sliding several feet and ending up wedged under my own car.

My injuries were severe enough that I required two surgeries and ended up with pins in my ankles and knees.

Love and light went out the window for a while and in their place, depression and self-pity took root.

I stayed in bed, asking God why this happened to me.

My parents picked me up for my doctor's appointment. I was in pain, physically and mentally, but did my best to hold it together, knowing that my tears would only bring on theirs.

That's when I saw her.

Sitting in the waiting room was the most beautiful woman. She was impeccably dressed, with an air of confidence that made you feel like you were in the presence of greatness.

And there I was, old sweatpants, stumbling along, fighting back tears. I felt worthless in her presence.

Until one sentence from her changed my perspective completely.

"You're so lucky," she said with a sad and wistful smile.

"Lucky?" I thought. "I'm currently a disabled, unemployed burden to my parents wearing the same clothes I wore to bed last night and this chick is calling me lucky?"

"Look at who you're here with," she said, "and look who I'm here with. I'm totally alone. I wish I were you."

I realized in that moment that my lowest, was someone else's greatest wish.

On my worst day, I still had something that someone else would give anything to have.

That lady snapped me right out of my funk, and I began to look for the blessings in this situation.

A couple months after my accident, Covid hit. Everyone I worked with in the mental health hospital was required to continue working. Many of them ended up with Covid, and some even passed away.

Had I not been in that accident, I would have been required to work even with my compromised immune system. I can't say I'm glad I went through it, but I found the miracle behind it.

Since I wasn't going to work every day, I had time to dive into advocacy work which gave me a new purpose.

If you're going through something difficult, it can be tough to look for the good in it. But I promise it's there.

I've come to realize that setbacks are not stop signs. They're just invitations to rest, regroup and find new ways to give, new reasons to be grateful, and new pathways to inspire.

DO MAIN CHARACTER STUFF

My God brother Kibwe used to say that everyone from Baltimore was "hood adjacent."

We are in the Northern most Southern State, so we have a bit of calm southern charm but we'll "knuck if you buck!"

He also always said that I had main character energy.

I wasn't sure what it meant at first, but then I realized that he was referring to my willingness to jump into the center of any story and make things happen!

He drowned on a mission trip in South America in 2016.

Not long after, I relaunched the brand Hood Adjacent Tees, both in memory of him and as a reminder to myself that if you want to be the main character, you have to do main character stuff!

If your life right now is tough or uninspiring, change your role!

Don't be afraid to tell your story. I'm not embarrassed about anything I went through. What may be "tea" for you, is a testimony for me.

If you're going to talk about what broke me, invite me to the table so I can tell you what God did with the pieces.

Imagine how boring movies would be if the main character wallowed in bed and never healed. Imagine how boring it would be if the main character settled into a life devoid of passion or meaning and you spent two and a half hours watching that character sit on the couch. You'd want your money back!

You are not an extra sitting in the background with no lines.

You are not a supporting character, whose relevance is derived from someone else's plotline.

No.

You are the main character. This is *your* plot. Your story.

Your chance to create a life of rich experiences, deep joy, and lasting impact.

Be the main character. Be the change. Be the reason someone else's faith in humanity is restored.

Be the soul in every room you walk into. Leave light in every room you walk out of.

Because true strength isn't just about how much pain you can take.

It's about how much love you can give.

About Patricia

For as long as she can remember, Patricia has had the hardest time describing herself when asked the question, "Tell me about yourself." Describing Patricia, Trish, Patty Lynn, or Lyric, depending on where you know her from, is more challenging to encapsulate in mere words than it is to keep up with all the things she does. There isn't a single term or title that adequately defines her identity.

Patricia is a daughter, a sister, a friend—a mother, a wife, a confidant. She is both retired and disabled, yet also a serial entrepreneur. Trish is a fervent advocate for social change, dedicated to being her Brother's and Sister's Keeper. Patty Lynn's daily activities can range from appearing on billboards for various national campaigns to quietly registering voters at PTA meetings then rallying for justice, as long as her health permits.

Lyric is a multiple cancer survive-HER, survivor of suicide attempts, and a huge dork. She can go from Glorilla to Pastor Mike G to Reba to Floetry to Led Zeppelin to complete quietness in the span of minutes. A comedian, crafter, loner, and the life of the party, who can be silent for days. A psychiatrist who needs therapy, a church girl who is an ordained minister and still needs Space and Grace. Patricia is a proud union member and a cheerleader for improving her city of Baltimore for its amazing residents.

Trish is the owner of Hood Adjacent Tees, a graphic design,apparel and home goods company named in honor of her beloved brother Kibwe who passed while teaching children in Costa Rico, and Tew Advocate, a Lobbying Firm dedicated to making tables in spaces where people aren't given a seat.

What binds everything together is her deep-rooted commitment to community service, a trait inherited from generations preceding her who possessed an unwavering dedication to giving back. Through it all, Trish is most proud to be the devoted mother of two of the most amazing young men, Mikyle and Spencer, who are her motivation for everything she does. While she was raising and teaching them, they were molding her and making her a better person. One day, they will remember her examples rather than her advice, so she makes certain to set great examples for them. Patricia credits Kyle and Spence for being the driving force behind her accomplishments and the shine behind her million-dollar smile.

CHAPTER 13

EMBRACING CHANGE

Finding Strength in Adversity

By Gwen Medved

L ife tests us in ways we could never imagine. Change, whether expected or sudden, is a call to action—a catalyst for trans-formation. It's always our choice how we respond, and our resilience in the face of adversity shapes our journey forward.

For me, betrayal was a recurring lesson. I faced the fear of letting go and found the courage to leave an unfaithful partner, choosing to be the champion of my own life rather than a victim of others' actions.

After years of infidelity and betrayal in my marriage, I finally embraced the opportunity to create a life where I honored myself. Letting go of a relationship built on dishonesty and disrespect was traumatic, but it was also the catalyst for living true to myself for the first time in thirty years. I realized how much of myself I had sacrificed for a "happily ever after" that was never real. How often have you disregarded your intuition or stifled your needs to achieve a goal? For me, it was marriage and a life where I played a supporting role, molding myself to fit a dream that ultimately cost me my authenticity.

I wanted a family where my kids felt supported and stable, a life that contrasted sharply with my own upbringing. To achieve this, I carved away pieces of my true self until there was little left. My husband's repeated affairs became the key to reclaiming myself. Filing for divorce was the moment I resigned from living my life for others and began living for myself.

Discovery and change are terrifying. Whether it's losing a job, receiving a shocking diagnosis, or ending a significant relationship, change upends our world. For me, the infidelity wasn't the hardest part—it was the lies. Trust was shattered, and my challenge was to relearn how to trust myself and believe in a good world filled with good people. I chose strength over living in a cage, and decided to walk into the unknown with an open heart.

The first step to embracing this strength is leaning into the gift of change. For me, it came when I discovered my husband's infidelity once more. Calling his hotel room and hearing another woman answer threw me into shock. When I confronted him, he gaslit me, serving partial truths and acting as if I was crazy. I realized I'd been living a lie. My own commitment to a monogamous married life blinded me to the truth. It takes two honest, transparent people to create a monogamous marriage and the happy white picket fence life I wanted so badly. Coming to terms with reality, I decided to reclaim my self-respect and my life. I learned that staying a victim would only take me out. Reframing my perspective on betrayal and change has made all the difference, allowing me to wake up each day in my new life with hope.

In the marriage, I systematically became as small as I needed to be to fit into an increasingly narrow space in my own life. My focus became solely on those I loved the most at the expense of my own needs. I lost touch with who I was before I became a wife and mother and began to identify with the functions and roles I played for others. My husband's repeated affairs ended up being the catalyst for my coming back home to myself and saying "to hell with this crap!" Filing for divorce was the bravest thing I've ever done, and it is the exact moment I took back my life. I've never looked back in regret.

On a drive from California to Colorado, my eldest daughter shared a story about buffalo and cows during storms. Buffaloes walk into the storm, knowing the fastest way out is through. Cows run from the storm, prolonging their discomfort and fear. By facing the truth of whatever is going on in our life, we are charging into the storm like buffalo, and we own our power. To trust anyone or anything, it is essential to rebuild trust in ourselves and follow our own inner guidance. So, what does transformation look like and what are some of the steps to go through as you start rebuilding a life after a massive change?

STARTING THE JOURNEY OF CHANGE: ACKNOWLEDGEMENT, INTENTION AND SUPPORT

1. Acceptance and acknowledgment

- Accept the reality of the situation. Whether it's betrayal, job loss, or another significant change, acknowledging what has happened is the first step towards healing.

- Allow yourself to feel the emotions. It's natural to feel a range of emotions including anger, sadness, and confusion. Accept these feelings as part of the process.

2. Setting intentions

- Reflect on what you want moving forward. What kind of life do you envision for yourself? Setting clear intentions can guide your path.

- Create a vision board or journal your goals. This helps in visualizing the change you want and keeps you motivated.

3. Seeking support

- Reach out to friends, family, or support groups. Surround yourself with people who uplift and support you.

- Consider professional help. Therapists and coaches can provide valuable guidance and tools for navigating change.

Timeline of Change and Transformation After Betrayal

1. Immediate aftermath (0–3 months)

- Shock and denial: You may feel numb or in disbelief. This is a natural defense mechanism.

- Seeking answers: It's common to want to understand why the betrayal happened. While closure is important, remember that not all questions will have satisfying answers.

- Self-care: Focus on immediate self-care. Engage in activities that bring comfort and solace.

2. Rebuilding (3–6 months)

- Emotional processing: As the initial shock wears off, deeper emotions like anger and sadness may surface. Allow yourself to process these feelings.

- Reconnect with yourself: Spend time rediscovering your passions and interests. Engage in hobbies or activities you may have neglected.

- Establish boundaries: Learn to set healthy boundaries to protect your emotional well-being.

2. Growth and renewal (6–12 months)

- Forgiveness: This is a personal journey. Forgiveness doesn't mean forgetting but rather freeing yourself from the hold of past pain.

- New beginnings: Start exploring new opportunities, whether in career, relationships, or personal growth.

- Reflect and reassess: Regularly reflect on your progress and reassess your goals and intentions.

4. Long-term transformation (1 year and beyond)

- Sustained growth: Continue to build on the changes you've made. Personal growth is an ongoing process.

- Embrace life fully: Open yourself to new experiences and relationships. Trust in your resilience and ability to navigate future changes.

TOOLS OF SUPPORT: MEDITATION AND MORE

Meditation: a path to inner peace

Meditation has been a life-changing practice and was foundational for me in the early days after betrayal. It helped me move through the fear of the unknown and find strength during the chaos of a life flipped inside out. It allowed me to face the biggest storm of my life with love and courage. Here's how to start:

1. Beginner steps

- Find a quiet space: Choose a quiet place where you won't be disturbed. It could be a corner of your room or a spot in nature.

- Set a timer: Start with just five to ten minutes. Gradually increase the time as you become more comfortable.

- Focus on your breath: Close your eyes and focus on your breathing. Notice the sensation of each inhale and exhale.

2. Guided meditations

- Use apps: There are numerous apps available like Headspace, Calm, and Insight Timer that offer guided meditations.

- Online resources: YouTube and other online platforms have a plethora of guided meditation videos suited for different needs.

3. Developing a routine

- Consistency: Aim to meditate at the same time each day. Morning or evening sessions can help start or end your day on a calm note.

- Create a ritual: Light a candle, play soft music, or use essential oils to create a calming environment.

4. Types of meditation

- Mindfulness meditation: This focuses on being present in the moment without judgment.

- Loving-kindness meditation: This cultivates feelings of compassion and love towards yourself and others.

- Body scan meditation: This involves paying attention to different parts of your body, releasing tension and promoting relaxation.

Additional Tools of Support During Big Change and Transformation

1. Journaling

- Daily reflection: Spend a few minutes each day writing about your thoughts and feelings. This can be a powerful tool for self-discovery and emotional release.

- Gratitude journal: List things you are grateful for each day. This shifts your focus from what's wrong to what's right in your life.

2. Physical activity

- Exercise: Physical activity releases endorphins, helping to improve your mood and reduce stress. Find an activity you enjoy, whether it's yoga, running, or dancing.

- Nature walks: Spending time in nature can be incredibly grounding and healing.

3. Creative expression

- Art therapy: Engage in creative activities like painting, drawing, or crafting. Art can be a therapeutic way to express and process emotions.

- Music: Listening to or creating music can be a powerful emotional outlet.

4. Building a support network

- Friends and family: Lean on your loved ones for support. Sharing your journey with trusted people can lighten the emotional load.

- Support groups: Joining groups with others who have experienced similar situations can provide comfort and understanding.

5. Professional help

- Therapy: A licensed therapist can help you navigate complex emotions and develop coping strategies.

- Life coaching: A coach can assist in setting and achieving personal goals, providing guidance and accountability.

For me, meditation was the pin that held my unglued life together when my fight or flight instincts had me in total chaos. It continues to be a life-changing practice, helping me control the fear of the unknown and find strength in uncertainty.

Choosing myself and cultivating a renewed sense of inner trust was a challenge. I had no vision for the future and no coping skills for the great adventure of learning how to be a me after being a "we" for thirty years. I had to figure out who I was outside of my roles as wife and mother. I was a stranger to myself. I'd grown comfortable finding happiness in making others happy, betraying myself to prioritize everyone else's needs. It was my daughters' ultimatum—that they would distance themselves from me if I chose to stay in my toxic marriage—that was the catalyst I needed to leave. Seeing their pain pushed me to choose a different life, releasing the illusion of the white picket fence.

Reflecting on my journey, I've learned that the greatest gift I can give my daughters is to love myself first. Living true to myself has created a beautiful backlash of love and a call to be self-focused, not selfish. *Real* love starts with *self*-love.

Perfectionism, procrastination, and lack of self-worth are cruel saboteurs of self-love. They keep us small and prevent us from showing up authentically in the world. I've learned to move past these false narratives, understanding that hiding behind them kept me safe from judgment and rejection.

Knowing who you are, what you value, and what you will tolerate is crucial for navigating change. Recognizing when you betray your values helps keep you on track. Here are ten questions to guide you:

1. What brings you the most joy and fulfillment?

2. What activities make you feel alive and inspired?

3. What qualities do you admire and strive to embody?

4. What relationships bring you happiness and satisfaction?

5. What core beliefs guide your actions and decisions?

6. What goals are most important to you?

7. How do you prioritize self-care?

8. What causes are you passionate about?

9. How do you define success and fulfillment?

10. What experiences have brought you the most meaning?

Reflecting on these questions helps align your life with your core values, guiding you through change and self-discovery.

SELF-CONNECTION IS THE KEY

How many times have you found yourself ignoring your own intuition and setting aside your needs to achieve a goal you believed was greater? For me, it was all about staying with a man who was unfaithful and living a life where I played a supporting role rather than taking center stage. Voluntarily. I chose a partnership that upheld traditional roles so I could be a hands-on mom to my daughters. More than anything, I longed to create a family where there was a mom and a dad, a home where my children could feel supported and stable. I wanted to be the mother I never had—present, devoted, and always available when needed.

This dream, shaped by my own childhood void, led me to mold myself into a version of my life that fit this ideal. I exchanged my authenticity for something I valued more. But in doing so, I relinquished the parts I loved most about myself until there was barely anything left of who I once was. Reconnecting to what was truly aligned to my values and desires was vital to healing my heart.

CONNECTION AND SERVICE

As the founder of The Success School for Women, an online platform for personal and professional development, and an advocate against child sex trafficking, I have found my true purpose. Working with thought leaders and producing impactful work would not have been possible if I had stayed in a marriage that stifled my soul.

I now dedicate myself to showing up honestly and serving others authentically. My work aims to share powerful proven strategies for growth and development based on the Success Principles that have been taught to me by my amazing mentor Jack Canfield, author of *Chicken Soup for the Soul* and *The Success Principles*.

Being certified in the Canfield Methodology and The Success Principles, as well as having trained with Jack for over five years, I know the life-changing results firsthand. I am the executive producer of *It's Happening Right Here*, an award-winning documentary film on child sex trafficking. I get to spend my time working with authors, thought leaders and entrepreneurs as they work to make the world a better place. Hours spent brainstorming and brand building bring me pure joy and feels like play for me. I wake up on purpose and inspired. My life honors my core value of family and today I have the freedom and the mindset to honor my daughters and my relationships with each of them in a way that I could not while married.

This wouldn't have been possible for me if I had stayed in my marriage. My hope for you, dear reader, is that you find the courage and strength to be brave enough to accept change when it shows up in your life, use it as a catalyst for growth and expansion, and believe wholeheartedly that what happens to you, is meant for you, no matter what kind of package it comes in. Here is to your best life.

About Gwen

Gwen Medved is a best-selling author, an entrepreneur, and an advocate for women and children, known for her deep commitment to family and impactful storytelling. Gwen works with individuals and companies dedicated to making a positive difference and is on a mission to inspire others to see the opportunities hidden inside every obstacle.

Gwen has been featured in *Forbes, USA Today, Women's Health,* and *Entrepreneur* magazine, and has appeared on ABC, NBC, CBS, and FOX affiliates nationwide, as well as Yahoo! News, CNBC, and MSNBC.

A member of The National Academy of Best-Selling Authors, Gwen is a recipient of both the EXPY and Quilly awards. She is the executive producer of the Telly Award-winning film *It's Happening Right Here,* which raises awareness about child sex trafficking in the US.

Gwen holds a BA from Purdue University and an MEd in counseling and human services from DePaul University. She is a certified Canfield Transformational Trainer, Values-Based Leadership Coach, Health Coach, and a dedicated advocate for women, children, and families.

In her personal life, Gwen enjoys traveling and spending time with family and friends in the Midwest and Santa Monica, California. Her goals include lake house living with backyard chickens.

CHAPTER 14

SUITCASE TO SUCCESS

By Colleen Unema

The morning of my eighteenth birthday, my parents handed me a suitcase and asked me where I planned to live.

I knew it was coming.

I was the youngest and had witnessed this moment more than once. The suitcase was, by now, a relic of family lore that marked the beginning of adulthood. I had watched as my older siblings each experienced this rite of passage, taking the suitcase from my parents' hands and walking out the door to forge their own paths.

Today, such a tradition might be labeled as harsh. But in my family, it was a gift—a testament to the faith my parents had in their children and the pride they felt for the responsible, independent people we'd become.

They'd always be there for us but handing us a suitcase was a symbolic act of trust, meant to infuse us with the confidence to fashion a life of purpose and prosperity.

I come from a family of entrepreneurs. My siblings, cousins, aunts and uncles all populated store fronts of main street and my family name was plastered on all the town billboards.

I grew up in the "break room" of my parent's store, sneaking donuts, cleaning the coffee pot, and mopping up the bathrooms. As youngsters, we played hide and seek amongst the boxes of inventory and our extended family picnics were a mix of volleyball, golf and long discourses about sales and the economy.

I became a schoolteacher. I taught high school and college science for nearly twenty-five years. It was a wonderful career, but I always envisioned an encore career and decided to open a laundromat.

Everyone tried to talk me out of it. "It's a cash business," they warned, "Don't do it."

But I was confident in my numbers, projections, and skillset to run a business.

Shortly after leaving my teaching job, I dove headfirst into learning everything I could about the laundry industry.

I wrote a business plan, opened the area's first eco-friendly laundromat and was so successful that the city awarded us the title of "start-up of the year" just nine months after opening.

Here's what I know—whether you're selling laundry services, consulting clients or repairing cars, there are five principles for success that never change.

Master these five principles, and you'll never go broke. Or if you do, you'll know *exactly* how to get it all back!

MICRO DECISIONS MATTER

I'd waited for this moment for years. I was a huge Michael Jackson fan, and he was finally coming to my city. At the time I was in high school and in addition to schoolwork and cheerleading, I worked a janitorial job after school.

After all, I knew in January of that year, I'd be handed my suitcase!

Every one of my friends got a ticket to the concert. They were forty-five dollars, which in 1979 was a lot of money. I was tempted to call off work and buy a ticket, but when I told my father he said, "Is that the best use of your money?"

I didn't go to the concert.

That would be the first in a series of tough sacrifices I made to move towards success, advanced education, and financial freedom.

Some people make decisions based on what they want *now*. Smart people make decisions based on what they want *most*.

Micro decisions matter.

A micro decision is a small choice that might seem inconsequential on its own, but that influences larger outcomes and shape our trajectories.

Long term success requires short term sacrifice. If you can train your brain to focus on the end results you want, and to measure every decision against that vision, you'll be much further ahead than your peers.

Years later I attended my high school reunion.

As I chatted with my old classmates, I noticed a trend. A lot of them were living lives that were riddled with anxiety. They were paralyzed by the decisions they made in their youth, drowning in debt, married to people who should have been passing flings, and spending money on material things that would never set their families up for generational wealth.

I realized then how important my micro decisions had been. Missing that concert was a huge lesson in discipline and taught a vitally important lesson.

You must be willing to sacrifice in a way most people *won't*, so you can ultimately live like most people *can't*.

LEARN TO TOLERATE ANXIETY

Over the course of my career, I've noticed that handwritten letters and table manners aren't the only things that have fallen by the wayside.

We've become a society that refuses to tolerate discomfort. Our willingness to be challenged is eroding and dealing with the anxiety of risk has become a lost art form.

Imagine if the great minds of the past couldn't bring themselves to get uncomfortable. We wouldn't enjoy any of the conveniences we enjoy today. Someone has to take a risk.

People tend to label anxiety and stress as negatives, but in my family, we were taught that discomfort is a side effect of moving forward.

Anxiety is better than complacency.

You cannot do anything life-changing until you broaden your capacity for discomfort. Great change *requires* it.

One night, my husband and I ran into my accountant and her husband. Her husband said, "My wife hasn't slept in weeks doing your books. How do you stand it?"

We were a start-up and as is typical for a start-up, the financial metrics were all over the place. Yet it never occurred to me to be anxious about it.

I told her she was not cut out for startups and hired a new accountant the next day.

And thank goodness I did.

A few days later I received a FedEx package that rocked our world.

A giant corporation in the laundry industry was accusing me of trademark infringement and I was being threatened with legal action if I didn't change my brand completely. I was forced to hire an expensive trademark attorney and told I would need to shut down my business while they battled it out in court. It was a huge blow. We had advertising plastered all over the city. Everyone knew our brand, and now I was being bullied into changing it.

I couldn't afford a lengthy legal battle. We'd have to roll over and rebrand.

I know for sure that the accountant who was suffering insomnia over my books couldn't have supported me through that legal struggle.

It was a blow, but there was no time for wallowing. The branding agency agreed to design our new brand at no cost.

In the end, the company that bullied me stole my ideas and franchised them.

But that's OK because I had learned the value of the next success principle.

THE OBSTACLE IS THE WAY—HOW A SAD EMOJI BROUGHT A BIG WIN

I left a stable job and opened a cash business no one thought could succeed. Then, days after being named "start-up of the year," I was forced to shut down or rebrand.

Can you imagine? We'd spent so much money to get the community to know us and now, our name would have to change.

I could have cried and given up. My husband knew I wouldn't do either of those things.

He hired a company to print a giant sad face emoji with a tear and hung it over my existing sign. We were flooded with phone calls. Everyone wanted to know why our business was crying!

At that point, we renamed our business Brio Laundry, which meant vitality and life in multiple languages. We advertised an open house re-launch event and invited the community to come to the store and learn the secret behind the emoji. We hired a DJ and caterer, clothed the staff in branded merchandise and revealed the new name to the guests.

Our customers knew the story now, supported us completely and our business never faltered.

Despite months of legal chaos and a total rebranding, there wasn't a single downward dip in our financial graph.

That's because our community doesn't just love our laundromat, they share our values. It's not enough that your customers know *where* you are. They've got to rally behind *who* you are.

ALWAYS HAVE A PLAN, AND A BACKUP PLAN, AND AN EXIT PLAN

It might sound counterintuitive, but there's strength and freedom in structure. Whether you're building a new business, growing one or working towards any goal, the best way to succeed is to build a plan and a non-negotiable commitment to following it.

As I was growing my businesses, I knew what I had to do

every day. Mondays were for marketing. On Tuesdays I focused on financials. Wednesdays were for dealing with legal paperwork. Fridays were for lunch with friends and social posts.

Designating which tasks are dealt with on which days is not only a mark of efficiency and focus, but it prevents you from getting overwhelmed and distracted. I didn't spend my Mondays panicking over the trademark bullying. I reserved that for Wednesday, the day designated for legal issues. Had I allowed the stress of that situation to creep into Monday, I would've been distracted from carrying out essential marketing activities.

A plan helps you know how to divvy up your resources, where you're heading, and how to measure if things are getting better or worse! It's also your safety net when everything goes south.

In 2019 I purchased a fledgling dry-cleaning business. Nine months later COVID hit.

Many people don't know this, but dry-cleaning chemicals are carcinogenic and outlawed in most of the world. America, however, still allows the toxic chemicals. I refused to use them. Sweden and Italy were using a healthy alternative and my business became the third in the United States to offer it.

I had started to remove all the toxic chemical equipment. When my landlord was required to test for perchloroethylene, the EPA got involved. It took an entire year to mitigate the space and we were forced to operate out of a warehouse.

I did what any well-prepared business owners would do. I turned to my Plan B. Because Covid restrictions prevented us from having employees, I did most of the labor myself, drove the delivery truck and cleaned the bathrooms. I took no money out, outsourced what I could, dropped our ad budget and sold anything we didn't need. I continued to pay my employees through the pandemic and when the governor finally gave permission to open, we offered health care workers free laundry services.

I always strive to run my business by prioritizing people, planet, then profit. When I live and lead within those values, I am always guided to the next empowering and profitable idea.

The employee shortage was a huge challenge for all business owners. I realized I needed a way to train new employees fast and developed an online university for laundry employees. About that time, a man who had heard me speak at a conference reached out. He had an idea to form a sort of Uber service for laundry and was looking for some guidance. Shortly after, he launched Aloha Laundry Life and purchased my online university. This allowed me to follow through with the next step in my plan.

I knew that any good business plan *starts* with an exit plan and works backwards, so when my son called and announced that he wanted to buy the laundry business, I was ready!

I knew from day one I would give that business ten years and then move on to something else, and that's exactly what I did.

I still act as a consultant for my son, but I spend most of my time working on the Executive team for Aloha Life Laundry, teaching in the University and working on projects close to my heart.

Plan A sets you up for growth. Plan B steps in to solve problems. Plan C, your exit plan, frees you to step into the next phase of your purpose.

Embrace Controlling Your Own Destiny

It isn't until I talk to other people that I realize how strong I've had to be.

I often hear things like, "I don't know how you did it," or "I can't believe you went through that," but it never occurred to me to give up.

I wouldn't have it any other way.

I see so many people shy away from taking control of their lives. How many times have you heard someone say, "That's not my responsibility!"

The word *responsibility* at its core simply means "the ability to respond." Who wouldn't want the ability to respond to their own life? There's nothing more empowering than being responsible for your own fate, your own reality and for how you engage with this one life you've been given.

At every moment you have a choice. You can be life's victim, cowering in a corner with every unexpected blow, or life's partner, walking alongside it through the twists and turns fully confident in your own ability to navigate the storm and land on your feet.

I credit my family with instilling in me a kind of raw courage. I credit the principles of success I shared in this chapter with helping me build a solid foundation sturdy enough to hold any change or challenge.

When I quit my stable teaching job to launch my first start up, I wasn't terrified because I had made micro decisions that built a financial safety net.

Since I'd learned to tolerate discomfort, I was one of the few small business owners in my area who didn't fall victim to panic during the pandemic.

When a huge corporation tried to shut me down, I'd already learned to lean into the obstacle, and became more successful than ever.

Life is funny. It will bless you, then take from you. It will be kind, then merciless. It will always, always, be changing.

I've always charged forward backed by an unwavering faith in God. It's not that I see the world through rose-colored glasses, but rather through the lens of faith. When the troubles come, they don't blow me off the course of my life of faith. I trust that I'm right where God wants me to be, learning exactly the lesson I'm meant to learn.

Which is why it's vital that *you* remain strong and remember that growth is always preceded by discomfort and that the best success stories are not stories of smooth sailing in a straight line.

They are stories in which an average human looks risk in the face and charges forward, triumphing over adversity not just once, but again and again.

That unrelenting attitude is part of my commitment to stay strong, to serve, to be an example of hard work and innovative leadership and to be willing to make decisions that might be uncomfortable, but that foster growth, community, impact, and ultimately, the freedom to live a life I love.

About Colleen

Colleen is a nationally certified science teacher, teaching in the sciences for nearly twenty-five years, from high school to university. Her award-winning career in education was populated with innovative student field work, grant writing, technology, and curriculum development. She was recognized for her development of the curriculum titled "Sportsman as Conservationist"—an outgrowth of that movement was the development of a high school women's Fly Fishing Club. Casting lines and catching fish was secondary to leadership development.

Business ownership was never far away. She grew up in retail with self-employed siblings and cousins too numerous to count. Retiring from teaching, she opened Brio Laundry, Cleaners and Commercial Laundry. Her business was awarded Start Up of the Year.

With a master's degree in education, her business plan read like a playbook. Indeed, even the impending sale of the business was in her plan, the exit plan was written first. No one could have been prouder than Colleen when her son announced he would succeed her in the business.

Her first work in retirement was to create an online university for laundromat employees to learn how to process laundry. Laundry University continues to help laundromat and dry cleaner owners with training and onboarding new hires quickly and efficiently. She wrote and created the entire curriculum based on her expertise. Colleen continues to teach online master's classes. She regularly shares her expertise at national laundry industry events.

She currently serves on the executive team of Aloha Laundry Life. She became involved with Aloha in its infancy. As it has matured over the last few years the premise remains the same: to empower entrepreneurs to own and operate their own laundry service business.

Colleen is currently at work getting her extended family's bedtime stories written, published, and narrated. These are fictional stories about two children, Frederick and Sally, living on the frontier in the early 1800s. The stories are sweet and calming for bedtime. She has taken the lead to move them from oral history to written word so they can be shared with more children.

Foundational and unwavering is her belief in God and the blessings of family life. She and her husband live on an island in Puget Sound. They have three grown sons.

Contact Colleen:

colleen@alohalaundrylife.com

www.colleenunema.com

www.frederickandsally.com

CHAPTER 15

HOLISTIC WEALTH

Exercising the Mind, Body, and Spirit
for Extraordinary Success

By John Bellave

Within the complex labyrinth of cells and vessels, a stunning regeneration is occurring.

The muscle lining, once inflamed and damaged, has restored itself to health. The vital organs, once burdened with the task of metabolizing unnatural ingredients, now bask in the ease of nourishment.

The vessels and arteries, once clogged, are open, once again pushing life-giving blood through the proper corridors. The brain is now clear, and the chambers of the heart, having been rescued from the poison of bad decisions, have regained their luster.

The lungs, now free of toxins, breathe in relief.

The entire body rests in a symphony of automatic performance, restored to the ultimate state of vitality and longevity.

And all it takes for this kind of total body rejuvenation is one simple decision.

To change.

And boy did I need to...

The last time I saw my brother, Chris, we argued. It was Christmas eve, and after a series of disrespectful comments, I threw him out of the house.

You can imagine my horror four months later when I got a knock on the door at 6 a.m., and the police told me that he'd committed suicide.

Years later, my mother was dying of cancer. She fought it and was in remission. After the cancer came back, she refused treatment, and I took that personally. How could my mother want to leave us instead of fighting again?

I was so resentful that I wasn't fully present with her during the final stages of life. There were so many emotions I wasn't willing to face.

Those two incidents produced a devastating blend of resentment and guilt that weighed on me like a cement block tied to my ankle.

I didn't have the tools to cope.

Instead, I distracted myself with unhealthy habits and turned inward, distancing myself from everyone who loved me.

I was losing my business, losing friends, and leaving a string of burned bridges in my path.

My family became disconnected and it's no surprise. I was treating my wife, Jo-Jo and my two daughters, Lauren and Amanda like a nuisance rather than a blessing and it wasn't long before the husband and father they knew was gone and in his place was a short-tempered emotionless zombie.

The more I suppressed my emotions, the more weight I gained. Sugary, greasy indulgences became the norm, which produced more pounds, which made me more miserable. My body, unable to fight my abusive habits, responded with high blood pressure, type 2 diabetes, and weak joints.

In the end, the weight of processed foods and unprocessed emotions was a heavy burden to bear.

I can't remember the exact moment I woke up from this hell, but one day it occurred to me that I was spiritually, morally, and emotionally bankrupt!

It was time to come back to life.

I listened to the book "Can't Hurt Me" by David Goggins. It completely transformed my thinking. Having two daughters and now a granddaughter, Gianna, I made up my mind that I'd do whatever I needed to do to be there for them.

At one point, my doctor gave me a choice—get on blood pressure medication or read a book. I chose the book. It was called *Starch Solutions* and was about the power of a plant-based diet. It made so much sense to me. In my hometown, there's a restaurant that serves Nick Tahou's Garbage Plate which includes two cheeseburgers, home fries, macaroni salad, and topped with greasy hot sauce. It was my last meal with meat. From that day on, Jo-Jo and I went vegan.

I then started incorporating intermittent fasting, hitting the gym six days a week, and doing yoga and sauna sessions.

I was up by 4:30 a.m. every day, on the peloton by 5 and sweating by 5:10.

Then, I added cold water therapy. My bloodwork showed tremendous change.

I was finally restoring my health.

It might seem like I'm endorsing extreme eating habits and brutal exercise regimens, but I'm not.

Because the reality is that those things are not the core of my success.

My life and body completely transformed but it didn't start with a treadmill and a salad.

It started with a *decision*.

A decision to stop abusing myself, and stop settling for a mediocre, joyless existence.

It started with a decision to want, get and be *more*.

My transformation was huge, but it wasn't about weight loss. It was about living a life that my God intended me to live.

Building the Right Muscles

Imagine that when you turn sixteen, you're given a car. It's brand new and in pristine condition. The catch is that it's the only car you'll ever get. When it dies, you don't get another one.

Wouldn't you treat that car with the utmost love and care, knowing that its functionality depended entirely on how you took care of it?

Yet we all know that we get only one life. We get one body, one soul, one shot in this lifetime.

Our experience of life depends on how we treat ourselves. So why do we treat ourselves so poorly?

We punish our bodies with poison and toxins.

We damage our relationships with harsh words.

We ignore our potential and throw away dreams, settling into an existence of obligations that hold no meaning for us.

We decide "it's just the way life is."

Except it doesn't have to be.

Life can be whatever we decide it is.

Today I'm the healthiest I've ever been. My relationship with my family is rock solid and my career is deeply fulfilling. As the CEO of Kathy Ireland Licensing, I get the opportunity to put people in business for themselves and help them change their lives.

You see we're an ecosystem. How we treat our physical bodies affects how our minds operate, which affects our emotions, which affects our relationships, which greatly influences our overall experience of life.

Now that's not to say we have control over everything.

But we can, at least, commit to keeping our side of the street clean, doing what's right and respecting the gift of life in every way possible.

It's not hard to know when we've gone off course. From an early age, we're taught to hold an internal barometer that tells us the difference between right and wrong. Right feels good, wrong feels bad. Wrong might feel good in the moment, but it will ultimately end in feeling bad.

We have this barometer but forget to use it. We react to life without thinking, and without weighing what we do against our own value system. Soon we're caught in a pattern of distraction, disconnection and habits that disrupt the flow of our ecosystem. By doing the next right thing, the next right thing follows.

That's why it's important to exercise all the muscles that create the foundation for a good life—physical, mental, emotional, and spiritual.

When you keep those systems healthy, you create a ripple effect of positive experiences that add up to one deeply rich existence.

Exercising the Mental Muscle

Every day, our brains are bombarded with a barrage of information. Social media, emails, advertisements, conversations, and work concerns overwhelm our minds.

There's no break for our brains as it works to make sense of it all and we end up mentally exhausted.

We get this way because again, we accept that this "is just how life is" and fail to use our brains intentionally.

We just take whatever garbage comes our way, and let our brains figure it out.

But the brain is capable of so much more than just processing information.

Our brains have the capacity to change our experience of life.

Now sure, we want to exercise our cognitive minds and I do so through reading, listening to podcasts, not watching the news and taking a social media hiatus now and then.

But the real exercise is in mindset work—positive, productive thinking and above all, *discipline.*

If you went to the gym for a month, you'd see results, but without discipline, you'd give up and be right back where you started.

Discipline moves the needle and pushes us to keep going when our mood tempts us to stop.

Recently, Jo-Jo and I participated in the 4X4X48 challenge. The idea was to run/walk four miles, every four hours for forty-eight hours straight.

We absolutely hated it when we were in the middle of it, but we felt a huge sense of accomplishment once it was over. So much so, we've done it a few times.

Once you participate in such a brutal exercise regime, everything else feels easier.

Need to prep and pull off an important meeting? Simple

Have a tough decision to make? I've got this.

When you train your brain for discipline and action, you're reminded of your massive potential and your results in life will show it.

Best of all, since your brain is wired to recognize patterns and strive to keep them going, your pattern of accomplishment will naturally lead to *more* accomplishments.

A daily commitment to thinking with intention is as important to your health as a good night's sleep. I place a high priority on quality sleep and have been monitoring my nights for over five years.

It sets a tone for how your days will unfold. You can tolerate whatever the world throws at your poor, overworked brain or you can commit to thinking intentionally with a good night's sleep.

It's a choice between living in default mode or by *decision*.

THE EMOTIONAL MUSCLE WORKOUT

Imagine sinking into a tranquil state of calm, your thoughts evaporating away. With every inhale and exhale you're breathing in love and releasing negativity.

As you lay in the sound bed, you're cocooned in a blissful state of sensory deprivation, the stress of the day melting away in a timeless void of quiet.

Meditation, breathwork and sound baths are an important part of my emotional workout regimen.

When you allow yourself the luxury of being quiet, the ongoing chatter of your brain takes a rest, allowing you to zero in on the truths of your daily interactions and intentions.

This allows you to manage your emotions from a much healthier state.

Our emotions are powerful catalysts. The good emotions propel us forward and the bad ones hold us back and can even destroy our lives.

Emotions left unchecked are like letting a bull free to run in a china shop.

Our emotions are reckless and immature. They're largely influenced by our past, which means we may find ourselves in a situation today but react from the emotional state of our sixteen-year-old self.

That's why mental workouts are important. They allow us to spot when our emotions are real and when they're unproductive residue from years past.

We exercise our emotional muscles by recognizing our own triggers but also through healthy expression.

At the gym, a muscle can't change shape if you don't move it. Likewise, your emotions need to *move*.

Emotions left unprocessed become like a still and putrid pond in your body, overrun with algae and devoid of life. Unprocessed emotions can block the efficiency of your body just as much as a clogged artery can.

A daily habit of quiet prevents you from responding without thinking, which raises your emotional intelligence.

Just as physical exercise strengthens the body, activities that nurture emotional intelligence cultivate empathy and self-awareness.

Not only do those qualities improve relationships, but they allow you to navigate life with ease.

THE SPIRITUAL BOOTCAMP

The health of your spirit profoundly affects your life.

When our spirit is nourished, we experience life as a gift. Most people confuse spirituality with religion, but you can have a healthy spirit without setting foot in a church.

Sometimes it's as simple as making choices that align with your character and surrounding yourself with people who share your values.

I've had the same business partner for eighteen years. I met Larry Kozin on the golf course. Through the years, we've been through the ebbs and flows of business, but our skill sets and values complement eachother and I trust him implicitly.

Our collective goal is to create millionaires and we're on pace to do just that. We've built an incredibly successful business based on these spiritual principles:

When you put yourself last, you come in first.

You have to give it away to keep it.

And treat others how *you* want to be treated.

I've been fortunate to help hundreds of people grow their businesses by coaching them to conduct their work with the spiritual principles of integrity, positivity, and discipline.

Principles pay.

I've found, over the years, that the health of my mind and spirit are directly proportional to the health of my bank account!

A Lifelong Journey

With the help of my beautiful wife, I've remained committed to my physical health. I know, however, that if I get lazy, my body will revert to its unhealthy state.

Health and fitness are not a phase. To be impactful it must become a way of life.

The same is true for your mental, emotional and spirit states.

They require lifelong attention.

David Goggins wrote, "*It won't always go your way, so you can't get trapped in this idea that just because you've imagined a possibility for yourself that you somehow deserve it. Your entitled mind is dead weight. Don't focus on what you think you deserve. Take aim on what you are willing to earn!*"

I love that advice. Don't focus on what you think you're entitled to or accept what's thrown at you.

Commitment is the key to creating a life you love.

Find a reason to be excited to get up in the morning. For me, Jo-Jo, Lauren, Amanda, and Gianna are my deepest *why*.

I think of them when I wake up. I think of the example I'm setting for them. I think of the behavior I'm modeling and the legacy I'm leaving.

I'll never *arrive*. There's no earthly end to this quest for a healthy ecosystem. It's an ongoing journey and one I'm grateful to be on.

One life. That's all we get. When the engine stops, so do we.

With that in mind, I hope you'll take great care of the vessel through which you live your life.

I hope you'll nourish your one body, train your one mind, and balance your one spirit.

And I hope you'll remember that every second of every day, you're in the driver's seat, with the power to speed up, slow down, change course and ultimately choose not just your destination but the scenery, music, and the passengers you pick up along the way.

Roll the windows down, let the wind move your hair.

The road will get bumpy. There will be obstacles in the way.

But you always have the power to decide—turn back and give up, or move forward and enjoy the ride.

About John

John Bellave is a visionary leader dedicated to transforming lives by empowering entrepreneurs with innovative products, lucrative business opportunities, and pathways to multi-faceted success. With eighteen years of dedicated service and a recent honor as one of the 'Top 30 CEOs in the United States,' John's expertise and strategic insight position him for impactful expansion into some of the most dynamic markets across the United States.

Eleanor Roosevelt once said, "A good leader inspires people to have confidence in the leader. A great leader inspires people to have confidence in themselves." John Bellave, CEO of kathy ireland® LICENSING, embodies this philosophy. His leadership style is characterized by fostering self-belief and confidence among his team and partners, setting him apart in the industry.

John leads with a commitment to long-term success, understanding that it is intrinsically linked to the triumphs of his team. He has meticulously assembled a group of seasoned, passionate leaders who share his vision and dedication. This elite team of veteran professionals and forward-thinkers is driven to propel the company to industry leadership, pursuing ambitious goals with unwavering enthusiasm while upholding the company's core values and integrity.

As an influential entrepreneur and dynamic speaker, John commands respect within the relationship marketing industry. Known for his effectiveness as a trainer and motivator, he inspires others with his strategic foresight and compelling vision.

John envisions a significant shift in the US workforce from traditional corporate roles to sustainable home-based businesses. He believes that his company offers a unique opportunity with its low overhead, highly profitable business model that accommodates various investment levels. "I see a major shift coming in the US from corporate hourly jobs to a sustainable home-based business which complements our ability to offer someone a solid, low overhead, highly profitable home business that suits any initial investment level," John asserts.

Mr. Bellave's innate desire to enhance the lives of entrepreneurs and his unwavering aspiration to help others achieve greatness is both commendable and inspiring.

CHAPTER 16

FROM IMPOSSIBLE TO INEVITABLE

Listening to Silent Stakeholders

By Muna Ali

The sky darkens into an ashen gray even though it's midafternoon.

Where lush greenery once grew, the ground is brown and barren. Where wildlife once thrived, the brush is bare. Nearby a river, once rich with life and flowing clear, is murky and devoid of living organisms, its pathway restricted by plastic and floating debris, its surface coated in a translucent and toxic film.

This alarming description serves as a reminder of what happens when the exploitation of the earth remains unchecked and disregarded.

Since I was a child, I resonated deeply with the principles of sustainability. I didn't know it at the time of course, and didn't call it that, but the urge to live intentionally, and to care for the earth and its inhabitants, was always at the forefront of my mind.

For nearly twenty-five years I have worked across sectors, markets, and cultures in delivering social, environmental, and digital impact. My key focus areas include women, water, and waste, employing leveraged play for systemic change. As a management consultant and industry leader, I have led large, long-term transformative programs for Fortune 500 companies, global foundations, not-for-profits, multilateral institutions, and governments that have positively impacted millions of people.

I've learned that sustainability doesn't start with a multimillion-dollar budget and a board meeting.

It starts with me.

A FAMILY AHEAD OF ITS TIME—AND CULTURE

The atmosphere of India in the pre-independence era was not one in which women were favored.

The patriarchy was more than a social structure. It was a pervasive dogma that determined the laws, customs, and decisions. Men were the authority figures, and women were cast into subordinate roles, their merit determined by their willingness to perform their duties as obedient wives, daughters, and mothers.

But not in my family.

In the chiaroscuro of life, I was blessed to be born in a family where the men are the stronger feminists. The tradition was started by my great grandfather, a prominent freedom fighter who believed that for independent India to succeed, its women must succeed. Yet at that time, circa 1920, it was nearly impossible for an Indian girl to receive formal education. In the conservative, patriarchal society, women observed purdah, experienced segregation, and were mostly expected to stay indoors. There were so many freedoms to fight for!

My great-grandfather, brave and unconventional, started the first girls-only school in his village. He worked hard to create a place in which girls could thrive, even installing bathrooms so that nothing could prohibit the girls from getting their fair share of formal education. My grandmothers graduated from his school in the 1930s while continuing to give their unalloyed support to the freedom struggle and later contributed to institution building for a free, modern India.

Typically, after graduation, the educational journey ended for women, who went on to get married and raise families. Again, my family championed alternative paths. My grandfather continued the tradition of prioritizing the education of women and my aunt received the first doctor of philosophy (PhD) in our family in the 1960s from a premier institute in science, technology, engineering, and mathematics (STEM). Decades later I received the second.

I would not be where I am today if it weren't for the men in my family, including my father. They had complete conviction in every woman's right to unshackle her mind, to chase her dreams and embrace her full potential. It remains an unwavering intergenerational tradition in the family.

From Impossible to Inevitable

I am certain that what started as a significant step in my family toward formal education for girls was not meant to be solely attributed to being a responsible citizen.

The focus on higher education, the push for financial and societal freedom, clearly indicated a vision for systemic change.

An interesting perspective on systemic change is provided by thought leader and author George Monbiot.[1] He shares that incremental change leads nowhere. Society is a complex system with two equilibrium states that it flips between. One is called *impossible*. The other is called *inevitable*. When systemic change happens, what seems impossible becomes inevitable.

When I was a young girl, permission to think for myself was a luxury many of my friends didn't have, and I relished my independence.

Mahatma Gandhi, or Gandhiji, as we affectionately call him, shared a timeless message of nonviolence, human rights, diversity, and inclusion. These are widely known and practiced. He also proposed progressive economic models that support the Earth and its regenerative and reparative capacities. Heavily influenced by Gandhiji's compelling vision, I became a vegetarian and adopted a more intentional lifestyle. I loved animals, but I soon came to understand that they were part of a larger ecosystem where the disenfranchised at the base of the pyramid and environment are also silent stakeholders.

Society and environment are both complex systems and face critical challenges. I knew I could make a much bigger impact if I started at the root of the problem.

BUILDING SUSTAINABLE AND EQUITABLE FUTURES

Achieving sustainable futures requires humanity to solve our most complex, systemic, and existential risks. If we are to address the world's critical social, environmental, and economic wounds, our responses must be applied to high-leverage points, where small interventions can result in large changes throughout the entire system.

One such example is the 2030 Agenda for Sustainable Development, adopted by all United Nations member states in 2015. It provides a shared blueprint for peace and prosperity for people and the planet, now and into the future. At its heart are the seventeen sustainable development goals (SDGs). They recognize that ending poverty and other deprivations must go hand in hand with strategies that improve health and education, reduce inequality, and spur economic growth—all while tackling climate change and working to preserve our oceans and forests. The SDGs are a clear example of systems thinking, which is instrumental to harnessing effective levers to enable widespread change across complex systems. While implementing them across geographies during the course of my work, I have seen that the nature of equitable futures is dynamic, but the big structural picture remains fundamentally the same.

It is immensely challenging yet satisfying work, as it fits in with the equity and inclusion framework I was raised with and allowed me to live my life principles.

That to me is success—knowing and living by your core principles.

LOOKING AHEAD

The pandemic hit my country with the same unrelenting sabotage with which it hit the rest of the world.

Like everyone else, I was unprepared for the chaos and uncertainty or for the many ways in which life would drastically change.

As I watched it all unfold, the media sharing frightening statistics of illness and death every single day, I couldn't help but ponder my own mortality. Something was stirring in me, prompting me to think about contributing professionally to recovery and resilience efforts and the impact I wanted to make at a more personal level. I often wondered aloud about the "new normal" and if we could ever get back to any kind of normal after the unprecedented disruption we were witnessing. Could we? Should we?

For me, the pandemic became a portal to a new mindset, and with it came the burning desire to broaden my legacy. I spent time reflecting on what I had done well and what more I wanted to do before another calamity came my way.

Lessons Learned

True growth requires a radical upgrade of thinking.

A growth mindset is everything! When we look at establishing impact, it may seem like a daunting task. Impossible almost and beyond one's imagination.

The most important thing to do is grow; in this case this is one of the few forms of growth that are actually positive.

I decided to become involved in various start-ups whose missions were aligned with my own. Driven by purpose, we empower and educate mission-driven individuals to cultivate twenty-first-century skills in sustainability, entrepreneurship, and technology. Another start-up seeks to catalyze the potential of women through leadership and economic participation.

All these start-ups recognize the rapidly evolving global landscape and help build skills that address complex issues for tackling tomorrow's challenges today.

Sustain yourself.

What I know now is that while sustainability refers to the earth's ability to maintain itself over through regeneration and reparation, on a personal level it refers to living with intention, even when it's unpopular or inconvenient. Having been in the domain for nearly twenty-five years, I've learned that sustainability starts with me. If you think about it, the principles of sustainability are inherent in each of us. Every healthy human being has the power to regenerate, to preserve energy, to endure even in the toughest circumstances. Like a forest that is determined to regrow after a fire, or the blooms that reliably push through the thawed ground each spring, we all possess the ability to replenish ourselves and the spaces around us.

You are your closest environment, your most important ecosystem. Only when you preserve and protect yourself are you fortified to preserve and protect the world around you.

Adopt a people-first mentality.

One of the fundamental pillars of sustainability that often goes unchecked is social equity.

When I am establishing my impact programs, social equity is always on top of my list. How many women and other disenfranchised groups from the base of the pyramid are working there? And how many of those are in senior positions? Are the wages fair? Is any group being discriminated against? Are the workplace conditions safe?

You might wonder what this has to do with sustainability, and the answer is *everything*!

Companies are run by humans, and therefore humans are the root system of every endeavor.

Having grown up in a family that nurtured equality, a people-first mentality is vitally important to me both personally and professionally. You don't have to lead a mission, but you must make it your personal mission to be fair and objective and do the right thing.

THE WORLD IS ROUND, AND THE ECONOMY SHOULD BE CIRCULAR

Our present economic system can be considered a "linear economy," built on a model of extracting raw materials from nature, turning them into products, and then discarding them as waste.

Do we really need a global economy that is *always* increasing?

If you take a minute to unpack what that means, you'll quickly realize that a rising economy often means an increase in production, which has a significant burden on the environment. If current trends continue, we would need three planets by 2050.

How do we manage to decouple economic progress from environmental destruction?

That's a question that I am constantly asking in my work, and it often boils down to ways that minimize waste and promote a sustainable use of natural resources, through smarter product design, longer use, and recycling, as well as regenerate nature. This is a circular economy, in a nutshell.

How can we practice this on our own?

The first example most people think of when they think of a circular economy is waste management, but a circular economy is in fact so much more.

We can start by being more intentional about our purchases. For instance, in textiles and fashion there are initiatives that employ regenerative agriculture to produce organic cotton and other natural fibres, using natural coloring and dye, thus ensuring higher quality and safer garments for the health of consumers and the environment. By producing higher-quality garments, clothing can also last longer and be repaired, thrifted, and recycled. When we proactively reach out for such items, our one decision helps tackle the problem of pollution and contributes to solving other complex challenges such as climate change and biodiversity loss. Super cool, isn't it?

Circular economy approaches are all around us. They can be employed in a number of different sectors, from textiles to buildings and construction, and at various stages of a product's life-cycle, including design, manufacturing, distribution, and disposal. We can be responsible consumers or distance ourselves from these kinds of considerations, but we must ask ourselves what kind of planet we want for ourselves and our future generations.

REWRITING THE TALE OF IMPACT

Our society has painted a funny picture of success. Just scroll through social media, and you'll see people flaunting mansions, private planes, and designer handbags. Yet I know people who are multimillionaires and live very simply. And I know people with very little who consider themselves a success.

Success is subjective.

For me the word denotes a happy life that is lived in alignment with one's values, character, and dreams.

In my world that means living in step with nature and being an active, concerned citizen of the world. I am at peace because I have cultivated my own framework of values, and I commit every day to living by it and to weighing the decisions I make against it.

I have traversed a fair distance on my sustainability journey, but there is so much more to do. My heart still goes out to all the silent stakeholders—who speak in a language that we choose not to fully understand. They may need our support, but we need them equally to live a balanced life.

What if we all committed to considering this every day, not just when disaster strikes or   when there is a tragic, viral picture of a seahorse holding a cotton swab?

But it isn't just the external ecosystem that needs our consideration.

What about your personal one?

Will you wait until disaster strikes to make the changes your heart is calling you to make? Will you pay more attention to who or what is using up your time and energy? Will you care for yourself enough to rest and renew and preserve your resources?

I hope you will, because in the end we are all one. We are all living in one giant ecosystem. It is an ecosystem of our own design, one that can promote local economies centered around holistic approaches and in the process nurture resilience, reciprocity, and respect between people and planet. We can make the impossible, inevitable.

When you think of those two things as dance partners, it's easy to be intentional with your choices, because you finally understand that one of the best ways to foster a healthier, happier world is to become healthier and happier yourself.

On a quiet evening when I share these thoughts aloud, I can hear my great-grandfather smile.

ENDNOTE

1.   Marie Snyder, "What Seems Impossible Can Become Inevitable," Medium, December 26, 2023, https://medium.com/through-the-fog/what-seems-impossible-can-become-inevitable-3069743db2a6.

About Muna

Muna Ali, PhD, is a sustainability practitioner. She is on a mission to craft a better story for our common future by delivering social, environmental, and digital impact at scale.

Recognized among award-winning pioneers of the global sustainability movement, Muna has worked across sectors, markets, and cultures in leading leveraged play for systemic change. Her key focus areas include women, water, and waste. For nearly twenty-five years she has served more than fifty markets across Asia Pacific and Europe in leadership roles. As a management consultant and industry leader, she has developed strategy and led large, long-term transformative programs for Fortune 500 companies, global corporate foundations, not-for-profits, and governments that have positively impacted millions of people.

During the pandemic she developed and implemented impact-first recovery and resilience programs for nearly ten million small- and micro business owners in Indonesia and Bangladesh, both of which are now part of living history.

She is the founding mentor for Tomorrow's University of Applied Sciences (ToU), an accredited, remote-first institution redefining education. Driven by purpose, ToU empowers and educates mission-driven individuals to cultivate twenty-first century skills in sustainability, entrepreneurship, and technology.

Muna shares a deep concern regarding the narrowing civic space, particularly for young women in the Global South. She serves as adviser-in-residence of LedBy Foundation, a Harvard-incubated start-up that seeks to catalyze the potential of Indian Muslim women through leadership and economic participation.

She supports her alma mater, the Indian Institute of Technology (IIT), as an adviser to IIT Startups.org, a nonprofit venture that supports interdisciplinary tech start-ups. IITs are currently ranked third, after Stanford and Harvard, in the number of unicorns produced.

An active conference speaker at scientific, sustainability, and tech conferences, Muna is a regular invitee to industry panels, conferences, and surveys. She writes and speaks on several platforms, weaving compelling narratives for keeping humanity at the center of growth and for urgently employing the power of collaboration to accelerate progress toward securing our common future.

Learn more:

LinkedIn: www.linkedin.com/in/muna-ali

employing the power of collaboration to accelerate progress toward securing our common future.

Learn more:

LinkedIn: www.linkedin.com/in/muna-ali